Between Women: Domestics and Their Employers

In the series
Labor and Social Change
edited by Paula Rayman and Carmen Sirianni

BETWEEN WOMEN

Domestics and Their Employers

Judith Rollins

Temple University Press
Philadelphia

Temple University Press, Philadelphia 19122

Published 1985
Printed in the United States of America

Library of Congress Cataloging in Publication Data

Rollins, Judith.
Between women.

Bibliography: p.
Includes index.
1. Women domestics—United States—Interviews.
2. Women domestics—United States—History. I. Title.
HD6072.2.U5R67 1985 305.4'364 85-8022
ISBN 0-87722-383-1

To my grandparents,

Edith and Izzy,

and the Wades

Acknowledgments

Support for the writing of this book has come from many sources. Forming the core of the support were Brandeis faculty members Paula Rayman, Gordon Fellman, Egon Bittner, Kurt H. Wolff, and Karen Fields who saw me through both the writing of my dissertation and the revising of it into this book with remarkable constancy of intellectual stimulation and encouragement. Paula Rayman and Karen Fields, in very different ways, provided the critical contributions; their empowering support and thoughtful comments strengthened and clarified my writing.

A number of others also contributed in significant ways: Hussein Abdilahi Bulhan and Alan Klein were extremely helpful in thinking through the dissertation; Carmen

Sirianni and Phyllis Palmer made invaluable suggestions for revising it into a book; Bonnie Thornton Dill began helping me out of her sense of sisterhood long before we met and has continued to be a source of inspiration, information, and encouragement; Stephen London and Elaine Hagopian extended themselves in innumerable ways, creating an environment in the Sociology Department at Simmons which enhanced my productivity and facilitated the completion of the manuscript; and Rita Oriani typed the manuscript quickly and accurately, often inconveniencing herself in order to make deadlines.

But my deepest debt is to the women—domestics and employers—who gave their time and told the stories that form the essence of the book. Their stories, which led me to entirely new places, into different worlds and other times, into joy and laughter and pain and sadness—their stories enriched me far more than is evident in this book. For their taking me on these journeys into their minds and their pasts, I am profoundly grateful.

And it was financial support from the National Fellowships Fund, the American Association of University Women, and Simmons College that made the entire project possible.

Contents

1 Introduction 5

2 The History of Domestic Service 21

3 The Work 63

4 The Women 91

5 Deference and Maternalism 155

6 Invisibility, Consciousness of the Other, *Ressentiment* 207

Notes 233

Index 256

Between Women: Domestics and Their Employers

1. Introduction

The Research Problem

In social science literature, there is in fact a good deal of writing on the social-psychological aspects of domination.[1] Yet, the overall discussion of liberation from oppression—whether political, sexual, or racial—tends to emphasize economic change as the most fundamental aspect of change toward more just social systems. Research on the critical importance of the *minds* of people in creating and maintaining hierarchical systems seems to have been accepted as a weak complement to that on the importance of material arrangements. Too weak, in my opinion: the dialectic between consciousness and the material world is not one between elements unequal in weight or importance.

Certainly economic rearrangements are entirely necessary for class, gender, and racial stratification to be eliminated. But my objective is to reiterate, as others have done before me, that the ideas, attitudes, thoughts, and emotions of people must also be examined, understood, and "rearranged" if the objectifying and exploitation of humans by other humans is to cease. Any effort to destroy relationships of domination must take the social-psychological dimensions of that domination into full account or, as history suggests,[2] any more egalitarian economic arrangements that are established will eventuate into only new hierarchical forms.

It is clear that the energy within people toward creating hierarchical social systems has been strong and omnipresent. The material conditions thus created further nurture this energy but are not the sole cause of its continued existence and strength. The conscious and unconscious minds of interrelating people and their interpretations of the *meanings* of the forms of interrelating also have the power to generate and perpetuate ideas of inequality. While the types of economic systems that have institutionalized inequality have been varied, all have included interpersonal rituals that somehow reinforced the desire for accepting the systemic inequality of entire categories of people. It is the forms, uses, and meanings of such interpersonal rituals, as expressed in the relationship between black female domestic servants and their white female employers, that are the focus of this study.

Examining this particular relationship allows me to explore the dynamics of a unique form of an important labor arrangement. It is important because domestic service has existed in all types of hierarchical social systems, suggesting that the occupation is both congruent with and useful to stratification. (If so, how? Might some of its value to hierarchies be non-material as well as material?) It is unique because in no other labor arrangement is it typical for both employer and employee to be female, both members of the subordinate gender of all societies. (Does the gender of the parties affect the social position of this archetypical service occupation and the content of the relationship between employer and employee?) And the interracial form of the arrangement deserves attention because it reflects the racial division of labor in the overall society, exemplifies a case of "occupational ghettoization," and typifies the cross-cultural pattern of the darker domestic serving the lighter mistress[3]—itself a reflection of the world-wide stratification pattern. (How do the racial attitudes of the women affect the relationship? And are interracial relations between women distinct in any way from those between men or between men and women?) Thus, examining the relationship between black female domestics and their white female employers does, indeed, afford an extraordinary opportunity: the exploration of a situation in which the three structures of power in the United States today—that is, the capitalist class structure, the patriarchal sex hierarchy, and the racial division of labor—interact. As Zillah Eisenstein has stated: "Women share an oppression with each other; but what they share as sexual oppression is differentiated along class and racial lines in the same way that patriarchal history has always differentiated humanity according to class and race."[4] Essentially, how class and race inform this female-female work relationship and the meaning of the relationship both to the women involved and to the larger society are the central issues to be addressed in this book.

While any employer-employee relationship is by definition unequal, the mistress-servant relationship—with its centuries of conventions of behavior, its historical association with slavery throughout the world, its unusual retention of feudal characteristics, and the tradition of the servant being not only of a lower class but also female, rural, and of a despised ethnic group—provides an extreme and "pure" example of a relationship of domination in close quarters. Unquestionably, elements present in this dynamic can also be found in other labor arrangements and other kinds of relationships. And this is precisely the value of this study: the potential for the findings to have applicability to and thereby enhance our understanding of other kinds of relationships of domination, relationships in which the psychodynamics of the domination might be obscured by the more impersonal, institutionalized nature of the domination (as in a bureaucracy) or by the emotional and social bonds between the parties (as in a marriage) but in which they are just as powerful in contributing to the perpetuation of inequality.

Methodology

My approach to this research was based on the simple and fundamental assumption that those who have lived an experience know more about it than those who have not. Thus, the ideas of women who have been domestics or employers of domestics form the core of this study. Because I had been neither before I undertook the research and had not been close to women who had been either, I deliberately approached the project without hypotheses or *a priori* theories. I tried to enter into the research as openly as possible and allow the patterns and theories to emerge.[5]

My focus on the women and their interpretations of their experiences dictated one of my three main methods of obtaining information: I conducted in-depth interviews with twenty employers and twenty domestics. (To be clear, "domestic servants," now called "private household workers" by the U.S. Census Bureau, includes "launderers, cooks, housekeepers, childcare workers, cleaners and servants."[6]) Additionally, I read primary and secondary literature on domestic service throughout the world, giving special attention to western Europe and the United States. And I worked as a domestic for ten employers in the greater Boston area for various periods of time. These three main sources of data were supplemented by a few auxiliary ones: I interviewed personnel of various kinds of agencies dealing with domestic servants; I worked along with domestics as their "cousin" in order to observe long-standing relationships; I interviewed a twenty-one-year-old white youth who had grown up with black "maids"; I interviewed a college-educated black woman whose mother had been a life-long domestic; and I conducted a three-hour group discussion with six domestics.

I began the field research process by working for a month as a domestic during September 1981. I chose to submerge myself in the situation before even designing the research in order to sensitize myself to the experience of domestic work and of relating to a female employer.[7] Based on that experience (especially my appreciation for the variety of types of relationships created by different personalities and the hints of salient issues of the interpersonal dynamics between mistresses and employees), I decided that forty interviews should yield a satisfactory picture of the complexities of the dynamics and the women's attitudes toward them. And I decided that my working for a total of ten employers should afford me enough familiarity with various styles of interaction to sufficiently enhance my understanding of the literature and ability to hear and comprehend the information shared in the interviews. I resumed domestic work in early November and continued to mid-May 1982.

I obtained my jobs by placing advertisements in city-wide and suburban newspapers. Each advertisement elicited far more calls than I needed. I chose my employers on the basis of two criteria: that they had had domestic help for at least two years (so that my personality contributed minimally to their way of relating) and that they be at home while I worked. Additionally, I took into account location, ethnicity, and income level in order to afford myself as balanced and varied experiences as possible. Some employers wanted interviews before hiring me; most were willing to make arrangements over the phone. In no case did an employer know I was doing research; I told them I had been doing domestic work for a number of years in another city and showed them letters of reference (written by me) if they asked. In all, I worked for ten employers: for seven of them I worked for four weeks, one day (from four to eight hours) a week; by one, I was fired after the first day for working "too slowly"; and for two, I worked six months, one day a week. These two extended periods of employment were designed to afford me the opportunity of being a part of longer-term relationships.

The forty "focused interviews" were conducted with interview guides, but my objective was to encourage the women to elaborate on the aspects of the relationship that were important to them.[8] Therefore, the guide was used sparingly, more to prod discussion than to direct it. By this method, I tried to encourage the emergence of unanticipated issues. I obtained interviews in various ways. To locate domestics, I visited low-income black churches and asked for volunteers, set up interviews from informal chats I engaged in on public transportation to and from my domestic jobs, and received referrals through the Boston chapter of the NCHE (National Committee on Household Employment), through a homemaker/health aide agency, and through a black women's social service club that had run a training program for domestics. To locate employers, I placed signs in health spas, passed out flyers at an upper-income suburban shopping center, and put advertisements in suburban newspapers. I often received referrals from interviewees to their relatives and friends who were also employers or domestics. Most interviews were conducted in the homes of the women but a few were conducted in other locations (on their jobs, in restaurants, and one over the phone). All agency personnel were interviewed at their places of employment.

The Ethical Issue

My participant observation as a domestic worker raised an ethical question. Deception was, after all, a fundamental element in this phase of the research. None of the ten employers for whom I worked knew I was doing research for a dissertation or even that I was a graduate student. I deliberately led them to believe I was a full-time domestic and had been one for a number of years. Deception is not unusual in social science research. And if there is no risk of harm or trauma to the subjects (as is typically the case in participant observation where one of the researcher's goals is to allow the situation to remain as natural as possible), it is not even controversial. But it does entail dishonesty; my research led me to repeatedly treat other humans, the subjects of my research, in a way I would have, under other circumstances, considered immoral. What justification is there for the research situation to change one's morality?

The ethical guidelines for the American Sociological Association and the American Psychological Association do not address the issue of deception *per se.* The concerns of both organizations are with protecting the physical and mental well-being of subjects and protecting their right to privacy. The "Ethical Principles of Psychologists" includes such general statements as: "Psychologists respect the dignity and worth of the individual and strive for the preservation of fundamental human rights."[9] But the Principles specifically exempt the kind of participant observation in which I engaged from including any obligation of honesty: "*Except for minimal risk research,* the investigator establishes a clear and fair agreement with the research participants prior to their participation, that clarifies the obligations and responsibilities of each" (emphasis mine).[10]

Likewise, the "Code of Ethics" of the American Sociological Association recognizes the potential for social research to interfere with human dignity:

> Sociology shares with other disciplines the commitment to the pursuit of accurate and precise knowledge and to public disclosures of findings. However, because sociology necessarily entails study of individuals, groups, organizations and societies, these principles may occasionally conflict with more general ethical concerns for the rights of subjects to privacy and for the treatment of subjects with due regard for their integrity, dignity and autonomy.[11]

But only two articles in the Code approach the question of deceiving subjects. The section on "Cross-national Research" includes this statement: "Researchers should take culturally appropriate steps to secure informed consent and to avoid invasions of privacy."[12] And the section on "Respect for the Rights of Research Populations" includes this: "The process of conducting social research must not expose subjects to *substantial* risk or personal harm. Where modest risk or harm is anticipated informed consent must be obtained."[13] Both codes avoid raising deception as an ethical question. Rather, as stated, the concern is with harm coming to the subjects and to protecting their right to privacy. (And in both codes, "privacy" appears to mean anonymity.)

On the issue of surreptitious research, most social scientists are apparently quite lenient. In his book *Ethics and Social Science Research*, for example, Paul Davidson Reynolds even goes so far as to infer that such research does unknowing subjects the favor of allowing them to contribute to scientific knowledge:

> A number of important, valuable research procedures may be used without the knowledge of the participants. . . . The potential for direct effects, either positive or negative, is minimal in covert research; this is primarily due to the participants' lack of awareness that research is being conducted. . . . The concept of informed consent (reflecting the right to self-determination) was developed to ensure that participants would not experience substantial negative effects without their knowledge and willing agreement. A low possibility for negative effects substantially diminishes the justification for informed consent. . . .
>
> There is ample opportunity for investigators to demonstrate respect for the participants' rights and welfare; covert research allows participants to make an effortless contribution to social science.[14]

Reynolds' leniency toward deliberate deception (when no risk to the subjects is involved) appears to be typical of the attitude of most sociologists. Such a research method is used routinely. Most of the sociologists with whom I discussed my participant observations raised no ethical questions and indeed encouraged the use of the method because it had the potential of yielding valuable data.

But a minority position does exist. Herbert Kelman was one of the first social scientists to raise ethical questions that are increasingly debated by contemporary social scientists. Kelman questions the morality of deception itself:

> Serious ethical issues are raised by deception per se and the kind of use of human beings that it implies. . . . We seem to forget that the experimenter-subject relationship—whatever else it is—is a *real* inter-human relationship, in which we have responsibility toward the subject as another human being whose dignity we must preserve. . . . We tend to regard [the research experiment] as a situation that is not quite real . . . and to which, therefore, the usual criteria for ethical interpersonal conduct become irrelevant. Behavior is judged entirely in the context of the experiment's scientific contribution and, in this context, deception—which is morally unacceptable—can be seen as a positive good.[15]

Whether one agrees with Kelman's condemnation of deception or not, the truth of his observations on the research process must be recognized. I did indeed change my ethics about interpersonal relationships when I systematically deceived my employers; my "usual criteria for ethical interpersonal conduct" were deliberately altered. And social scientists do this all the time. Kelman sees this aspect of social research as part of a larger trend:

> We are living in an age of mass societies in which the transformation of man into an object to be manipulated at will occurs "on a mass scale, in a systematic way, and under the aegis of specialized institutions deliberately assigned to this task." In institutionalizing the use of deception in psychological experiments, we are, then, contributing to a historical trend that threatens values most of us cherish.[16]

Social scientists, then, are on both sides of the deception question, and in the middle. The fact that deception is employed so frequently in research indicates its acceptability as a method. So why, then, am I discussing it?

Because of my uneasiness with the idea when in the planning stages, an uneasiness increased by the probing questions of Dr. Kurt H. Wolff of Brandeis University. And because during the field work I felt guilt about what I was doing, particularly on those occasions when employers were open and human toward me. The guilt came from my compromised sense of fair play (and that is why it was stronger in relation to more humane women than in relation to the more exploitive).[17] But the deeper unease came from what I thought my actions might do to me as well as from what I was doing to others, and from my concern about the long-term ramifications of the systematic use of deception for a discipline and for a society that so easily objectifies human beings. For to dehumanize others is to dehumanize oneself; to treat others as objects is to make oneself more of an object. Something of my human spirit, however minute a something, would be lost, compromised in this process. The immediate question became: is what can be gained worth the loss? I decided it was. I decided that because this occupation had been such a significant one for low-income women and because so little research had been done on it despite its presence throughout the world, the understanding that might be gained by my putting myself in the position of a domestic, even in this limited way, was worth the price.[18] But it is important, I think, for social scientists to evaluate each research situation, to keep such questions under discussion, to recognize that deception is an ethical issue and that each time it is employed a personal and social price is paid. Therefore, deception must not be a research method to be taken for granted and institutionalized as entirely acceptable.

How did it get to be as acceptable as it is? Partly because the social sciences are Western disciplines and the West has been characterized by what Kelman calls "the transformation of man into an object to be manipulated at will."[19] I do not think it too strong a statement to say that the objectifying of humans that some social scientists practice springs from the same psychological source as does discrimination, exploitation, and genocide. The source is the ability to define the other as less than fully human, as separate from and other than oneself, and as, therefore, not deserving of the treatment that one would afford members of one's own, fully human, group. Thus I do not quite agree with Kelman that social scientists' use of deception is "contributing to a historical trend that threatens values *most of us cherish*" (emphasis mine). We are indeed part of a historical trend but our cherished values are in keeping with that trend: most social scientists, like most other Americans, value success and achievement above honesty and humaneness. Not unlike the entrepreneur who has one set of ethics for his personal life and a very different set for business dealings, the social scientist often uses questionable methods to gain good data, the key element to success in his or her field.[20]

The deception and manipulation of others that takes place in social science reflects, reinforces, and contributes to the dishonesty and manipulation of people in the larger society.[21] This is not something social scientists need to encourage by institutionalizing it. The repeated loss of pieces of their own humanity will ultimately result in poorer-quality social science. And "there is something disturbing about the idea of relying on massive deception as the basis for developing a field of inquiry. Can one really build a discipline on a foundation of such research?"[22] Most important, social scientists' unquestioned reinforcement of the subject-object *Weltanschauung* of the West contributes to the continued human deterioration of a society already spiritually bankrupt.

The form of my exposition of findings, too, has been influenced by my emphasis on the women who have been part of the employer-domestic relationship. Throughout the following chapters, I attempt to allow the women to speak for themselves whenever possible. The chapter that follows is an overview of domestic service throughout (mainly Western) history and in a few non-Western locales. The chapter concludes with a rather detailed history of servitude in the United States with emphasis on the South and the Northeast, the areas most relevant to this study. The third chapter describes conditions of work—the physical labor, hours, compensation, advantages, and problems. And the next three chapters—Chapters 4, 5, and 6—form what I consider to be the heart of the book: these chapters focus on the women and what emerged as the major dynamics of the relationship between them.

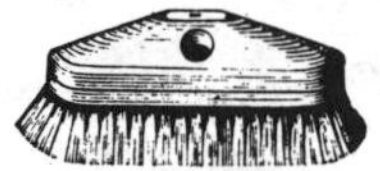

2. The History of Domestic Service

Overview of Origins

Domestic service, in all but a few parts of the world, is now associated with women. And the origins of domestic work throughout the world are with women. Male slaves, and later serfs and employees, who have done domestic work at various times and places in history were, in fact, a later development. The popular conception of domestic slaves as the original household workers misses this important fact: slaves were originally taken to supplement or take over the responsibilities of women.

The position held by the women of a tribe determines to some extent whether or not slaves are wanted. Where all

> the drudgery is performed, and can be performed by the women, and men do not want to relieve them of it, there is not great use for slave labour. But where women enjoy high consideration, the men are more likely to procure slaves who are to assist the women in their work.[1]

The evidence is, indeed, that the earliest slaves were used for household labor.

Slavery was prevalent throughout the ancient world. And where slavery existed, some slaves were used as domestic servants. There is written evidence of slavery in Sumeria (as early as the fourth millennium B.C.), in Babylonia, and among the Hittites, the Hebrews, and the Egyptians. Although slavery existed in Greece at least as early as 1200 B.C., the supply and demand reached its peak during the fourth century A.D. when almost a third of the population of Athens was slaves. Throughout this period, "women slaves were used in household services, with the customary accompaniment of concubinage."[2]

The wars of conquest under the Roman Empire brought an immense supply of slaves. The large number led to a high degree of specialization, including secretaries, musicians, masseurs, tutors, slaves in charge of perfumes, of silver drinking vessels, of brooches and pearls, and slaves whose job it was to dress and look well. (As will be seen, domestics, being used as status symbols has existed throughout history.[3]) The essentiality of slaves in the Roman household is evidenced by the language: the word for household, *familia,* was derived from *famulus,* which meant house servant or domestic slave.

Both agricultural and domestic slavery declined in Europe from about 900 to 1300 A.D., when "serfdom was better adapted to the crude and non-commercial agriculture of central and northern Europe."[4] But there was a marked increase near the end of the Middle Ages because of invasions of eastern Europe, Italian slave-trading with the

Turks (in Armenians, Syrians, Bulgarians, and Serbs), the Spanish dispelling of the Moors, trade in Sudanese by Arabs, and the Portuguese importation of West Africans. Throughout this period, the church made no attempt to abolish slavery and in fact held slaves. Domestic servants at this time, then, were made up of both serfs and slaves.[5]

The Moslem world used exclusively slaves as domestic workers. In fact, "household slaves rather than field slaves were the rule."[6] Female slaves there, too, might also be "concubines of their masters, with a special and stable situation in the family if sons were born."[7] Islam, like Christianity, tolerated slavery, particularly of non-believers.

In India, "domestic work was the occupation of Sudras and slaves not only in the ancient period but also throughout the mediaeval ages right up to the nineteenth century"[8] until slavery was abolished in 1843. The domestic slaves and Sudra servants of Moghul India were mainly female, often used for "luxury and display," treated abysmally, and commonly sexually exploited.[9] The two reasons given by Indian sociologist Aban Mehta for the degraded position of Indian domestics have cross-cultural applicability:

> The slave is looked down upon as belonging to a physically weaker or socially inferior race to whom the members of the more powerful race have delegated the burden of heavy and disagreeable work . . . owing to cleanliness taboos and notions of spiritual contamination associated with certain functions which are held in contempt. Thus almost all the functions performed by slaves come to be associated in the minds of men with weaknesses and subordination and hence the degradation to all forms of slave labour.[10]

Manual, dirtying labor has been held in contempt in the West, of course, as well as in India; and slaves have always formed the lowest strata in any hierarchy in which they existed. Although throughout the world all domestic servants were slaves at some point in the past, it is noteworthy that in certain areas (India, the Arab countries, and the United States, for example) that point was actually quite recent.

This brief overview of domestic servitude in selected parts of the ancient world has yielded glimpses of the origins of a number of issues still important in domestic service today: the origins of household work are with women; there has been a tradition throughout the millennia for female domestics to be used sexually; housework is manual labor and manual labor is universally denigrated; and, until very recent times, there has been an association between domestic servitude and slavery.

But while domestic service—that is, non-family members performing household maintenance functions—has been ubiquitous, it is in feudal and industrializing western Europe that the roots of the American domestic service tradition lie. Let us, therefore, examine in some depth domestic servitude during these periods.

Domestic Service in England and France

Before the Industrial Revolution, domestic servants were mainly in the households of the aristocracy. In such households, domestic servants might "run into the hundreds" and were always part of a multi-layered staff of servants. Only in the homes of village churchmen, prosperous farmers, and a few substantial merchants might one find a few servants or a single servant maintaining the household. And before the nineteenth century, nearly as many men as women did indoor domestic work.[11]

Through the Middle Ages and even during the Industrial Revolution, the most desirable positions for domestics were those in the large homes of the aristocracy: "For most servants in medieval England the best chance of assuring for themselves comfort and security . . . was to obtain a position in the household of a noble family."[12] These positions varied greatly. The gradations among domestic servants were distinct and complex, based mainly on the nature of the work performed. The principle demarcation was between upper and lower domestics. The former were "executive and supervisory" personnel of some skill and special training; the latter were directed and manual workers of little skill. This categorization meant differences in wages, living conditions, food, dress, use of leisure time, amount and quality of contact with the employer, and, of course, prestige.[13]

At the top of the servant hierarchy, managing the estate, was the land steward or, if the land holdings were small, a house steward who managed both land and house. Close in eminence to the house steward was the gentleman-in-waiting, the "confidential advisor and personal attendant" to the head of the household. And of equivalent rank to the gentleman-in-waiting was the master of the horse, handling the stables and all the liveried servants who worked in the stables (including the coachman, helpers, and boys). Other upper-level men were the clerk of the stables, the clerk of the kitchen, the man-cook, the confectioner, the baker, the bailiff (who handled all aspects of agricultural buying and selling in addition to sometimes serving meals), the valet, the butler, the gardener, and, lowest of the male upper servants, the groom of the chambers (who specialized in furniture maintenance). The lower, liveried male servants included the coachman, the footmen, the groom, the underbutler, the undercoachman, the park-keeper, the gamekeeper, and a number of young men with titles such as postilion, yard boy, provision boy, foot boy, and page.[14]

There were three female positions considered upper level: lady's maid, housekeeper, and cook. Though in training and capabilities the housekeeper was equivalent to the male house steward and the female cook to the male cook, in each case the males ranked higher and the women's authority over lower servants was limited to female servants. The lower-level female servants included chambermaids, housemaids (cleaners), maids-of-all-work, laundry maids, dairy maids, and, at the bottom, scullery maids (responsible for cleaning the kitchen, the dishes, and all cooking utensils).[15]

The differences between the lives of servants at various levels in the hierarchy were vast. For example, it was not unusual for an eighteenth-century house steward to make £100 a year, while the laundry and dairy maids began at £2 and reached a maximum of less than £10 a year. (Note that in both England and France, male servants always cost more than female servants and were, therefore, more of a status symbol.) Upper-level servants might have separate sleeping quarters with "pillows, bolsters and mattresses," but lower servants "were expected to sleep on sacks of straw spread out in the hall or attic,"[16] dormitory-style. The degrading livery was confined in the eighteenth century to only lower-level male servants. The quality and amount of food, as well as separate eating tables, also distinguished the upper from the lower servants. And it was to the lower-level servants that the stigma of servitude was most fully attached; they were seen as people who were "valueless to the community, . . . who contributed nothing to the common welfare, . . . and whose position was conceived to be but a step or two removed from serfdom."[17]

The Traditional Master-Servant Relationship

The salient feature of the servant's position before the changes caused by the Industrial Revolution was that he or she was considered fully a part of the patriarchal household, expected to give the same loyalty and obedience and to receive the same protection and guidance as would a family member, particularly a child. Indeed, "in both the French and English language, in the seventeenth century, 'household' and 'family' were synonymous terms."[18]

This view of household relations was in the tradition of the Roman *patria potestas:* the male head had ultimate power over and responsibility for all the people in his house—wife, children, and servants.[19] (It should be recalled that in the Roman context, domestic servants were almost always slaves since "few free men or women were willing to perform the menial labour which domestic service entailed."[20]) The term "paternalistic" is repeatedly used by writers to describe the traditional master-servant relationship.[21]

A blatant manifestation of this view of servant as household and family member was employers' casual approach to payment of wages in seventeenth- and eighteenth-century Europe. Although servants were "hired" for an agreed-upon wage, records of seventeenth-century and eighteenth-century France and England show that some wages were seldom paid, some were replaced with articles of clothing, and often payment was treated in a cavalier manner by employers: "The practice of paying a servant only a small sum (or in kind—with clothing, etc.) and allowing his wages to fall into arrears is found before 1750 in all types of households and all levels of the servant hierarchy."[22]

This paternalistic philosophy and limited use of wages also had the effect of keeping servants in one position for long periods of time. On the other hand, servants could expect far more than room and board; eighteenth-century guides for proper behavior of a gentleman toward his servants indicate the employer was responsible for their morality, for their religious direction, for their total material welfare (including medical care when ill), for their care when too old to work, and even for making provisions for them in his will. In return, servants were expected to give all of their time to their master, to relinquish all thought of having private lives, to give total obedience unless "ordered to do something contrary to the dictates of the law of God or the law of the state," and, critically important, to give total fidelity even to the point of defense of the master and his family.[23] As the most widely read guide in seventeenth-century France on the proper relationship between master and servant, Claude Fleury's *Les Devoirs des Maitres et des Domestiques,* put it:

> [Masters owed their servants] not only temporal subsistence, but instruction, good morality and spiritual benefits. . . . [And the servants'] first duty is fidelity. This is the foundation of all social intercourse between men and especially of domestic society, which cannot survive without the confidence that a patriarch has in his wife, his children, and his servants.[24]

The traditional paternalistic relationship between master and servant was, then, both consuming and protective of the servant, far more than the contractual arrangement that was its legal basis. Its core was in the tradition of patriarchal domination, a type of domination the essence of which was the respect of tradition (a belief on the part of both master and servant in the rightness of the relationship) and the personal bond between the two parties. Max Weber offers this description of the basic characteristics of patriarchal domination:

> Essentially, it is based . . . on a strictly personal loyalty. The roots of patriarchal domination grow out of the master's authority over his household. [This] personal

> authority [finds its] inner support in the subject's compliance with norms . . . [which] derive from tradition; the belief in the inviolability of that which has existed from time out of mind. . . . The master wields his power without restraint, at his own discretion and, above all, unencumbered by rules, insofar as it is not limited by tradition or by competing powers. . . . The two basic elements of patriarchal authority then are piety toward tradition and toward the master.[25]

Lest the reader romanticize paternalism, it should be kept in mind that the master "wielding his power without restraint" could and often did entail brutality and degradation as well as protection. Punishment for laxness, a transgression of deference, or insubordination was often physical: "servants of both sexes were liberally caned, cuffed and slapped." Cases of brutality to the point of death were reported even in the nineteenth century and, as elsewhere, sexual exploitation of female servants appears to have been commonplace.[26]

There were variations and exceptions, to be sure, but paternalism, with its complex system of life-supporting and life-destroying elements, may be justly used to describe the nature of the typical master-servant relationship of pre-industrial western Europe. The expansion of the middle class with the rise of industrialism, however, changed that relationship profoundly and irreversibly.

Domestic Service in Industrializing England and France

The period of industrialization in western Europe was the period in which the largest percentage of the labor force was engaged in domestic service. The number of domestic servants in England increased steadily in the nineteenth century, reaching a peak in 1891 with 1,549,502 domestics.

France peaked earlier in 1881 with 1,156,604 domestics. "Thus, the English and French patterns follow a generally similar path in the course of the nineteenth century, although the French servant population kept better pace with the general population increase than did that of England, and peaked earlier."[27]

The highest concentrations of domestics were in urban areas: 21.5 percent of all English domestics were in London in 1851; 20.1 percent of all French domestics were in Paris in 1891.[28] Domestic service was the "major setting for female urban labor force participation during the transitional stages of industrialization."[29] Interestingly, this is also the period of the highest overall unemployment of women:

> At an earlier stage a high percentage of all women work, largely as unpaid family workers in agriculture and artisan handicraft. . . . At a later stage, as in the United States in recent years, the proportion of women working again rises as married women increasingly seek employment.[30]

The key point is, however, the continual and dramatic increase in the number of household workers until the last decades of the nineteenth century.

Why this increase? Why the association between a growth in the domestic service sector and the rapid expansion of industrialization? Who were the "new" domestics? What effects, if any, did the increase have on the quality of the relationship between employers and servants? And for what reasons did the numbers in domestic service decrease at the end of the nineteenth century and continue to do so into the twentieth century? I will try to answer these questions fully, if succinctly, because many of the experiences of nineteenth-century western European domestics as a labor group in relation to the overall society and as employees in relation to their employers have applicability to the later experiences of domestic servants in the Third World and the United States.

The domestic service sector of the labor market increased during the nineteenth century for two basic and complementary reasons: increased industrialization created a larger middle class, which could afford to hire household help, and changes in the agricultural sector pushed large numbers of young people into the cities to seek employment. Beginning near the end of the eighteenth century but accelerating in the mid-nineteenth century, the western European middle class was rapidly "transformed, renewed and enlarged" by an influx of formerly lower-income rural people, uncertain in their new status and anxious for the rewards and symbols of success.[31] Having household help came to be viewed as an altogether necessary element of their lives: "Middle class life can scarcely be conceived without the servants. To know the number of families served by domestics allows one to as exactly evaluate the number of middle-class families."[32] An income of merely £150 a year would enable a family to employ one servant.[33] This meant that the new employers of domestics included not only large merchants, bankers, industrialists, and the like but also small tradesmen such as "drapers, grocers, plumbers, coal merchants, corn dealers," et cetera.[34] One newspaper's claim that "there is scarcely a mechanick in town who does not keep a servant in livery" might have been an exaggeration but suggests the reality that servants were seen as appropriate by even the less than affluent—appropriate and, because of the plentiful supply, affordable.[35] And an additional factor contributing to the increase in demand for servants was that increasing numbers of middle- and upper-class children were surviving to maturity.[36]

Though the aristocracy remained a vital and emulated element of society, it had always been a small percentage of the total population and during the nineteenth century, because of "the increasingly high cost of maintenance, the replacement of the autarchic castle and the manor house . . . by the country seat, . . . and the effective suppression of the serving-men,"[37] its households, in fact, diminished in size. It was not, then, from the traditional western European retainers of domestics that the increasing demand came, but rather from people new to the role, trying to imitate the aristocratic lifestyle, to be sure, but bringing to the position a new style, different demands, and the uneasiness of the novice.[38]

Simultaneous with the growth of the middle class were stresses in the rural demography and economy that forced numbers of young people into urban areas for employment. The children of farmers, "together with those of agricultural servants and labourers, comprised the chief source of supply" of domestics.[39] French peasants reacted to their overpopulation by "siphoning off . . . excess children into domestic 'apprenticeships' outside the area"; advancements in agricultural technology lessened the need for farm workers; the "law of settlement . . . forcibly expelled or encouraged the migration of all who seemed likely to become chargeable"; and the English enclosure movement displaced renters or reduced them to laborers.[40] At the same time, the city held out its usual lures to young people: the promise of higher wages, greater possibility of upward mobility, freedom from family discipline, and the excitement of urban life. Thus the largest portion of domestic workers came from the countryside.[41]

A few urbanites did go into the occupation, especially into positions requiring special skills. It was not unusual for children of artisans, manufacturers, tradesmen, and lesser clerics to be placed in domestic service. And there were rare cases of servants imported from abroad.[42] But the attitudes of both the urban middle class and the urban lower class checked the voluntary flow of the latter into domestic service.[43] The middle class considered the urban lower classes dangerous, "vicious and dishonest, hence entirely unfit for service." Children of the extremely poor typically became "matchsellers, hawkers, flower girls, and too frequently thieves and worse." And lower-class urbanites clearly avoided domestic work whenever possible; though comparable in pay to other occupations involving physical labor, it retained the stigma of servitude and could be perceived as an acceptable choice "only if one preserved certain values of dependence that the city did not breed." Thus an urban-born servant of lower-class background was a rarity,[44] and throughout the nineteenth century, the principal source of the burgeoning domestic servant sector was the countryside.

The Master-Servant Relationship in Industrializing England and France

The changes in the composition of the employing and servant groups during the nineteenth century had various ramifications in terms of the quality of the master-servant relationship. The term "master-servant" itself became less appropriate than ever before in history: servants were hired to supplement or take over what were considered the wives' responsibilities and during this period middle-class wives came to have primary responsibility for the hiring, deportment, and work assignments of servants.

An even more significant change was the "feminization" of the domestic servant labor group itself. Although almost half of the domestic servants of mid-eighteenth-century France and England were men, by 1850 domestics in both countries were predominantly women. Because this process has cross-cultural applicability, Theresa McBride's concise explanation of it is quoted *in toto:*

> This pattern [in England and France] fits a characteristic model for industrializing societies. In general, during the

> intermediate stage of economic development, the personal services sector is very large; urbanization creates a demand for service personnel in bars and restaurants as well as in the homes of the newly-rich entrepreneurial class. Domestic labour becomes commercialized and absorbs a large segment of the unskilled labour which migrates to the urban centers. Gradually, however, the men move into the modernizing sectors of the economy, leaving the females confined to the service sector by restrictive social values and by their lack of training. The women are slower to leave service for other employment, and consequently, the service sector is largely feminized at this stage.[45]

And as the occupation became more female, the size of the typical servant-employing household became smaller. The middle class, less affluent and more urban than the aristocracy, could not maintain large staffs. There was "a continuous reduction in the number of servants per household . . . during the transitional stages of industrialization" and the houses with one "maid-of-all-work" or a few servants became commonplace.[46]

This physical change had two important effects: it contributed to the "derationalization" of household work and it put greater work demands on the few servants present. Because servants were now expected to do multiple household tasks, rationalization of work was precluded. At the very time that other sectors of the economy were experiencing an acceleration of rationalization, "a derationalization of the domestic economy occur[ed] as fewer servants [were] asked to undertake a wider range of jobs."[47] Most nineteenth-century servants, then, though gradually receiving higher pay, had excessive work demands placed on them as middle-income families strove to meet standards set by the gentility. Charles Booth suggested that a minimum of three servants—a cook, parlormaid, and housemaid—were necessary to run a London house efficiently; yet over 30 percent of the domestic servants he located in his turn-of-the-century study of London worked alone and another 25 percent were in two-servant households.[48] What emerges is a picture of a new type of master-servant relationship: typically female and far more tense and intense than that of the eighteenth century because of the lower numbers of servants per household, the smaller quarters in which people lived, and the greater demands placed on each servant.

The degree of tension between employer and servant heightened for other reasons. A fundamental one was the newness of the majority of people in both groups to their positions: the men and women of the new middle class had not dealt with servants before and the young people from rural areas had no training nor models for appropriate servant behavior.[49] Though most servants were of the same ethnicity and religion as their employers, distance between the two increased as the members of the new middle class strove to separate themselves from their domestics by drawing rigid class lines. During the nineteenth century, a plethora of writings supporting the divine origin of class position and manuals on the proper management of domestics appeared. More elaborate symbols of deference were demanded, and by 1850 even the use of livery—always perceived as degrading by servants—was required for most female domestics.[50] This need for greater deference, for clearer class distinctions on the part of the middle class, undoubtedly grew out of their insecurity and upward striving. Employers of the new middle class used their domestics to help define their new class identity. There was no shortage of articles and columns written about the various negative aspects of servants' speech, dress, work habits, unfaithfulness, morality, et cetera, the basis for which may have been both real and a result of the need of the middle class to differentiate themselves from this group, which lived in such close physical proximity. Some historians believe that it was during the nineteenth century that masters and mistresses began to consider servants less than human.[51] Yet the demand for servants continued to increase into the latter part of the century—despite higher wages, their supposedly low morals, inadequate performances, and lack of proper subservience.

The uneasiness with the occupation increased with servants also. The best indicators of this were the increasing turnover rate throughout the nineteenth century and the steady decrease in the total number of domestics near the end of the century as alternative positions became available. The servant-for-life, not unusual during the seventeenth and eighteenth centuries, became rare. By the late 1800's in England, "a minority remained as servants all their lives, some experienced 10 to 15 years of service and then married; some left after a short time."[52] But other signs of discontent included efforts to organize (which focused, interestingly, more on improving conditions of work than on higher wages), a successful campaign against legal physical punishment of servants, increase in forms of passive resistance (wasting time, impudence, sulking, et cetera), and an increase in petty thievery in the last half of the century.[53]

The changes at the end of the century that eventuated in a rapid depletion in the numbers of domestic workers and near elimination of those "living in" by the second decade of the twentieth century have to do with both the occupation itself and the changes taking place in the larger society. Alternative job opportunities became more available and acceptable. For female servants, the issue of acceptability of certain occupations had retarded their exodus from domestic work. Though factory positions had been available earlier, western European social values held that there was more respectability in domestic work because of the supposed protection, the opportunity to save money, and the potential for training for marriage. In England, "girls and women did not make the transition to other occupations . . . easily."[54] Social ideology (which decreed that the natural place for all women was the home) and lack of opportunity conspired to keep them in service positions. However, by the late nineteenth century, this ideology was weakening and women were following male servants into other occupations. The fact that the white-collar sector was expanding facilitated women's escape; white-collar employment was less demanding physically and was considered entirely as respectable for women as employment within the home.[55]

Popularization of the concept of citizenship also contributed to servants' discontent with their positions. Though they desired rights afforded those in other occupations, full citizenship was not accorded western European servants until the late nineteenth century or early twentieth century "on the grounds that anyone in this dependent child-like employment was not a responsible adult, hence any extension of suffrage to them would merely reinforce the political power of the established elites."[56]

Changes in the middle-class household and attitudes also contributed to the diminution of domestic work, particularly of the full-time, live-in type. Rising costs (of rent, food, and domestic help), weariness with the conflicts and tensions of the relationship, the decreasing size of middle-class families, improved household technology, and a change in values that emphasized privacy and familial closeness, all contributed to more and more middle-class women making "the difficult choice not to employ a live-in maid."[57]

And, finally, the spread of public education and literacy during the last half of the nineteenth century increased servants' awareness of themselves as workers, instilled a desire for more independence than live-in servitude afforded, and gave servants skills that "expanded their occupational options."[58]

These social, technological, and attitudinal changes converge at the turn of the century to mitigate against the continued expansion of the domestic servant labor force. The gradual decline that began then in western Europe and that was accelerated by the economic changes caused by World War I has never reversed itself.[59]

Domestic Service in the Non-Western World

In the work of English-speaking historians and social scientists, there is a dearth of material on domestic servitude in the non-Western countries during the periods of European conquest and colonization. That the European colonizers used domestic servants drawn from the conquered population is clear from personal journals and fiction. That such a labor group shared features typical of domestic servants everywhere (low pay, long hours, low status) may be assumed. However, the effects of the uniqueness of the situation—the political and economic dominance by force of a large indigenous population by a foreign minority—on the master-servant relationship may only be guessed at.

There is, however, enough material on the non-Western world during the twentieth century to enable us to glimpse contemporary trends. As might be expected, since these countries are at various stages of the industrialization process, they are exhibiting a fast rate of increase in the percentage of the labor force engaged in domestic service and this sector is becoming increasingly feminine. But the reader is cautioned against assuming further generalizations are appropriate based on the industrializing parallel: a

Third World country of this century is not in the same position as as an industrializing country of nineteenth-century Europe either in terms of its relation to the world order or in terms of its history and goals. Domestic servitude in the very diverse non-Western world is extraordinarily varied in its characteristics, numbers, social position, and content. Latin America, India, and South Africa have been chosen for detailed discussion because of both the amount of scholarship available on them and their representativeness of varied patterns in domestic servitude outside the Western world.

Latin America

Latin America "leads" the Third World in both the size of the domestic service sector and the percentage of women in the occupation. In her survey of twenty-one Third World countries, Ester Boserup found that only in Latin America did women constitute over 90 percent of domestics throughout the continent. "Paid domestic service is an important female occupation in both rural and urban areas of Latin America," more important there, possibly, than in any other part of the world.[60]

This fact is closely linked to a unique characteristic of Latin American urbanization: more women than men migrate into the cities, resulting in urban populations having more women than men and rural populations having the reverse.[61] This flow of female migrants creates a large, cheap labor pool. Not surprisingly, recent migrants are more likely to go into domestic work than either earlier migrants or urban-born women. A 1970 study of Santiago, for example, found that "nearly two out of three recently employed migrants but only one in five earlier migrants and one in nine natives" were in domestic service positions.[62] And a 1971 study of domestics in Lima concluded that nearly two-thirds of recent migrant women who entered the labor force went into domestic work.[63]

The fast rate of urban migration in Latin America and the demand for domestic servants mutually affect one another, for "employment opportunities and continuous flow of migrants stimulate each other: the former favor the continuity of the migratory flux, and the later guarantees a comparatively cheap labor force which, in turn, stimulates the demand for labor and the emergence of job opportunities in [the domestic service and construction] sectors."[64]

Two other significant effects of the abundance of cheap domestic labor worthy of note are on the social infrastructures of Latin American countries and on the personalities of middle- and upper-class family members. Some of the services provided by domestics in Latin America are necessitated because there are no other provisions for accomplishing them (for example, paying bills downtown, shopping for all household items, and carrying mail to and from the post office). The presence of such a large number of servants eases the pressure on private companies and the government to add costly services to their activities. For example, the post office need not extend its services as long as domestics are available to handle pickup and delivery.

> The existence of a household servant class is a major factor . . . in subduing the impetus to make changes . . . not seen as really necessary as long as the needs of the people are presently being taken care of. The very existence of a class of household servants retards . . . the process of organizational efficiency.[65]

The other important effect of such a large domestic force is more difficult to measure. But a number of writers mention the dependency of members of the middle and upper classes that develops as a result of a lifetime of being served. The effects of this are manifold. Nett discusses the life-long child role of those reared by servants: "The child takes over adult functions vis à vis other adults, but remains niña (child) or señorita (miss) to the servants, even when a matron or grandmother. . . . The patron may make decisions, but he could never operate his farm without servants, as a North American farmer can."[66] Yet the servant, too, as in other parts of the world, is viewed as a child and Nett speculates that this perception of servants as irresponsible children carries over to other employer-employee relationships in Latin America, further "retarding the development of workable organizations."[67] The presence of servants also precludes the necessity of the development of daycare centers and tends to isolate the child. And,

> if the servant has the primary tasks of caring for children up to adolescence, the ideal type of middle class American character structure would be less likely to develop—especially if the child was shielded from the universalistic morality of games (formal rules and technical competence) with serious peer competitors. His situation is still the norm in middle and upper class Latin American families thus producing adults, especially males, with well fed egos but poorly prepared for an objectively competitive university education.[68]

An additional characteristic of the domestic servant sector in Latin America is that it is composed disproportionately of people of Indian or mestizo backgrounds.[69] To my knowledge, however, there has been no research on the ramifications of the servant group's being of a different racial (and often religious and language) group from the employer. Researchers have, however, commented on a not-unexpected aspect of this heavily female household servitude: sexual exploitation and "semi-prostitution [seem] to be widespread among the group of domestic servants" in Latin America.[70]

Domestic service in Latin America, then, exhibits the increasing numbers and high feminization expected of an industrializing area. But, in addition, it was seen that the exceptional size of this sector affects both the social infrastructure and the personality development of the classes served.

India

India has had an ancient tradition of domestic servitude, though up until the abolition of slavery in 1843, all domestics were either slaves or Sudras.[71] The tradition had been so strong, in fact, that one writer has concluded that the large number of servants in Indian cities today is "no modern phenomenon, but is in fact an attenuated survival of the fashions prevailing in the time of Akbar and doubtless dating from a much earlier period."[72] Though some slaves of that period were imported from western Asia and Africa, most were captured in raids within India or entered slavery "voluntarily" because of debts or famine. Neither the Hindu nor the Moslem religions objected to the institution of slavery, and it survived into the colonial period until abolished throughout the British Empire.

Domestic servitude in India in the mid-twentieth century shows many expected characteristics: domestics are mainly in cities, their numbers are increasing rapidly, it is an extremely low-paid and low-status occupation, and it is composed mainly of migrants from rural areas. However, unlike those in Europe and South America, domestics in India are mostly male. This is untypical even of other parts of Asia.[73] The reasons have to do with migration patterns and female participation in the labor force. More men than women are migrating into cities, and in urban India only 17 percent of adult women "have any gainful activity beyond work in the household." (Contrast this to the 25 percent to 35 percent of urban women in the labor force in Latin America.[74])

As of the 1951 census, there were a total of 1,424,000 domestic servants in India, constituting 4.4 percent of the labor force in other than agricultural occupations. Bombay, typical of Indian cities, showed a steady increase in the number of servants in the first half of the century.[75] A 1960 study of Calcutta found domestic servants constituting one of the two largest and fastest-growing occupational categories (along with shop owners). And, in both cities, the excess of men encourages prostitution within and outside the servant class.[76]

Sociologist Aban Mehta's explanation for the migration of rural Indians into the cities has a familiar ring: "Extreme poverty, insufficient means of agriculture and lack of employment in their native places compel these people at a young age to leave their families behind and come down to Bombay in search of jobs . . . ; [however,] domestic work is distasteful to almost all of them."[77]

A hierarchy among Indian domestic workers exists, less elaborate than that of eighteenth-century England but perhaps even more rigid because particular jobs are associated with particular castes and religions. On the top of the pyramid are the housekeepers and butlers, with gardeners and cooks in the middle, and "general help" (including cleaners, launderers, errand boys, et cetera) in greatest numbers (51.2 percent), doing the "more arduous and unpleasant tasks" and receiving the lowest wage. In 1951, Mehta found that the average male servant in Bombay worked a 12.4-hour day and the average female servant worked a 7.8-hour day. Typically, the men received half a day off once or twice a month, but 20 percent were never given leave. Average job tenure for both sexes was about five-and-a-half years. The issues brought up most frequently as sources of dissatisfaction were the loss of liberty, the irregular working hours, and the lack of future prospects in domestic work. Yet Mehta found no efforts to organize among Indian domestics and his explanation for this lack is insightful. He speculated that five factors mitigate against organization of domestics: the lack of homogeneity in the group and the fact that they work separated from one another; the personal and sometimes intimate relationship between employer and employee, which makes workers consider organizing inappropriate; the privileged positions of some domestics, which they would not want to threaten; the perception of many workers, especially women, of their position as temporary; and the "apathy, ignorance," and pervasive depression among domestics because of their low-paid and low-prestige jobs.[78]

Thus, domestic service in India demonstrates characteristics observed in Europe and Latin America: this industrializing country has a fast-growing and increasingly urban domestic service sector. Cultural traditions have retarded but not stopped the feminization of the occupation but in all other important aspects—low wages, long hours, low prestige, the occupation resorted to by the least skilled, least assimilated group in the city—domestic service in India reflects world-wide patterns.

South Africa

As in India, domestic servants in most of Africa and all the Arab countries are predominantly male. In none of these areas is the servant sector as large as in Latin America, but it is increasing in size. The reasons for the predominance of men varies by area: in India, it is because of the greater involvement of and need for women in agriculture; in the Arab countries, it is because of the traditional prohibition against women engaging in any kind of economic activity; and in Africa, it is a result of colonial restrictions against the urban migration of women, women's extensive involvement in agricultural activities, and African men's discomfort with their women working for a non-family male.[79]

South Africa is an exception. As in Latin America, domestic service in South Africa is an extremely important occupation for women and affords the employing population an extensiveness of service with low levels of payment rare elsewhere. With people of color (Africans, "coloreds," and Asians) constituting the majority of the population and with domestic service the most common occupation of both African and "colored" women, it is not surprising that South Africa has the highest number of domestics as a percentage of all adult women (12 percent) and of all women in non-agricultural occupations (52 percent).[80] The availability of cheap domestic labor means that almost all whites, including those of lower incomes, have household help.[81]

And this has been the case since Europeans arrived in South Africa. Records as far back as 1777 show that the early Dutch settlers employed and enslaved members of the indigenous population—usually Khoikoi or San and often male—for domestic work.[82] This system of domestic servitude was interrupted by an influx of immigrants from England, many of whom were domestics, which began in 1820. For the next half century, there was a large component of Europeans in the domestic servant sector. But as alternative jobs became available, Europeans left domestic work and were replaced by Africans; "by 1890, domestic service had been transformed into a predominantly black, female institution."[83] And it has remained so, typically an arrangement between a white employer and a "colored" or black employee. The relevance of this institution in South Africa to this study is obvious.

Working conditions for domestics in South Africa are, on the whole, consistent with the nation's treatment of its non-European majority. (This is part of the reason that South African writers have called the institution a "microcosm" of the society's racial situation.[84]) A 1974 survey of the members of two progressive organizations revealed that 31 percent gave no vacations to their live-in domestics, 49 percent gave no public holidays off, 49 percent provided no heat in servants' rooms, and 30 percent provided no bath or shower. Average payment was 14.5 cents an hour.[85] In their 1969–70 study of three areas of Durban—where most domestics are "colored"—Whisson and Weil found wages for live-in help ranging from 6.17 to 12.9 cents an hour; for live-out servants, from 9.49 to 15.5 cents an hour. The live-in help averaged over fifty-six hours work per week; full-time live-out help averaged thirty-seven hours per week.[86] And in 1978 and 1979, Jacklyn Cock found in the Eastern Cape that over 31 percent of domestics worked seven days a week, 22.9 percent got no paid holidays, full-time domestics worked an average of fifty-nine hours a week, and wages ranged from R4 to R60 a month, averaging R22.77 a month.[87] All of the 175 domestics she interviewed had some dependents (averaging 5.5 per domestic), and 58.3 percent of them were the sole support of their families. Cock concluded that few employers "pay their domestic servants a living, let alone a just wage."[88] The overall picture is one of long hours, inadequate living conditions, poor food, low pay—in Jacklyn Cock's word, "ultra-exploitation." However, there is one positive feature unique to the occupation in South Africa. Because of the government's apartheid policy, the Immorality Act, outlawing interracial sex, tends to protect domestic workers from the kinds of sexual advances made by male employers in other parts of the world. Though it is not unknown, researchers have found this type of exploitation to occur minimally.[89]

The relationship between the South African employer and her servants is one of gross inequality based on a number of factors. The most obvious are color and class but not to be ignored are other stratifying factors such as language (English is considered superior to Afrikaan and Xhosa), place of origin (urban-born is superior to rural-born), and, of course, the low prestige of servitude itself.[90] This inequality is reinforced by having domestics wear uniforms, by having them address employers as "master" and "madam" while the employers use first names, and by the presence of some of the more demeaning aspects of paternalism (gift-giving, treating servants like children) with few of the traditional protections.[91]

Domestic service in South Africa functions in much the same way as elsewhere: services are provided that release the employing women from household activities, status is afforded the employing family by the presence of servants, and some amount of assimilation into the culture of the employing group is afforded domestics. However, because of the close caste-job association in South Africa, it has been suggested that the omnipresence of servants in white South African homes serves another important function: the justification of apartheid. The servant is often the only contact white South African women and children have with "coloreds" and blacks, and because "the expansion of opportunities in industry and commerce [has] . . . drawn off an increasing proportion of the better educated and energetic non-whites," the required obsequiousness and often genuine ignorance of domestics (because of rural or educationally deprived backgrounds) support the prevailing belief in the inferiority of "coloreds" and blacks:[92]

> The humble domestic servant, dropping a cup at the end of a 10-hour day, whispering "Master" and "Madam" when summoned, perpetually insolvent, occasionally drunk . . . is the dependant whose homage is balm and honey, the instrument which frees her employer for the good life and the justification for apartheid.[93]

Domestic service in South Africa is an extremely significant institution. Because its size and composition affect the qualitative aspects of the entire lives of the domestics and their families and the lifestyles and attitudes of the employers, it thereby both reflects and contributes to larger structures—particularly those related to racial and sexual domination—in the society.

Domestic Service in the United States

Though one might expect domestic service in the colonial and early American periods to share commonalities with that of England, it was in fact a very different phenomenon on this side of the Atlantic. Early settlers brought with them democratic ideas that undermined their comfort with the traditional paternalistic master-servant relationship. Yet the domestic servants of the colonial period were various types of unfree or indentured laborers. Thus, from its beginnings, domestic servitude in this country has embodied a kind of contradiction between principles and behavior that did not exist in seventeenth- or eighteenth-century Europe, a contradiction between the value of egalitarianism and the actual class and caste stratification. This tension has always "contaminated" the master-servant relationship here, but it will be seen that it has been more significant at particular periods and with particular groups of people in our history.

A second distinguishing characteristic of the U.S. experience is its diversity: domestic service in the North was and is quite different from domestic service in the South; and the later development of this labor group in the Midwest and Far West, too, took distinctive forms. Because the women who are the focus of my study are historically connected to the Northeastern and Southern experiences, particular attention will be paid to those two areas of the country.

There are four distinct phases of servitude in the United States: the colonial period, the period from independence to about 1850, the period from the mid-nineteenth century to World War I, and the "modern" period from World War I to the present.[94] During the colonial period, service was performed by "transported convicts, indentured white servants, 'free willers,' negroes and Indians."[95] England found the policy of ridding herself of undesirables by sending them to the colonies extremely attractive; in fact, it has been claimed that the "principle reason for colonizing these parts [was] to give an outlet to so many idle and wretched people as they have in England, and thus to prevent the dangers that might be feared from them."[96] The largest number of convicts and indentured servants went to the middle and southern colonies but they were found everywhere, including New England. Free willers—Europeans forced to sell themselves into slavery to pay for their passage to America—were found only in Maryland. Indeed, these European servants (who, at the time, were distinguished from Indian and black servants by the word "Christian") outnumbered servants of color in Virginia and Maryland until the end of the seventeenth century.[97] Indian servants were most numerous in New England, and black servants, in the South. What is noteworthy about this period is that the line—both legal and experiential—between "servant" and "slave" was quite unclear: "In every section negro slavery grew up side by side with white and Indian slavery."[98] Though servants of European descent had slightly more legal protection, journals and legal documents of the day indicate that all categories of servants were treated poorly; work conditions—housing, hours, food, et cetera—were often wretched and physical brutality commonplace.[99] Servants were not free wage-laborers; they were all of classes and/or races considered biologically inferior; liberal democratic principles simply did not apply to them. However, this pre-Revolutionary period was the one in which Northern and Southern servitude were the most similar. Toward the end of the eighteenth century, new patterns began to emerge, patterns that polarized domestic service in those two sections, making the institution more dissimilar than it had been or ever would be again: black enslaved labor began to displace white servitude in the South and native-born free laborers displaced Indians and indentured whites in the North.

This second period, from the Revolution until about 1850, includes both the most egalitarian master-servant arrangement (in the North) and the most dehumanizing one (in the South) in the American experience. The Revolution had popularized democratic ideas and as native-born whites replaced foreign or "colored" servants in the North, that is, as free wage-earners supplanted indentured or slave labor, "the social chasm that had existed between employer and employee diminished; the term 'help' was almost universally used; there was an absence of liveries and all the distinguishing marks of service and an intolerance on the part of both employer and employee of servility and subservience of manner."[100]

Very often the servant would be of the same community, ethnicity, and religion as the employer. This and the fact that they were wage-laborers caused them to be perceived as "socially the equal of their employers."[101] Thus the term "servant," associated with unfree labor and the demeaning European class system, was abandoned.[102] Livery remained absent. Though this unusually democratic form of servitude was short-lived, the later servant class's knowledge of its existence and familiarity with the philosophy of equality on which it was based affected their attitude toward the institution; and this, in part, caused the tensions collectively described in housewives' manuals and popular magazines as the "servant problem." It is clear that, in employers' minds, such democratic treatment was not appropriate for immigrants, and as their numbers increased toward the mid-nineteenth century, this form of servitude became limited to the diminishing numbers of rural, native-born servants.[103]

Simultaneously, black slaves displaced almost all types of white domestic workers in the South. This close association of the inferior occupational and social status with the lowest racial status—the addition, as Du Bois would later say, of "a despised race to a despised calling"[104]—had the effect of both reinforcing racial prejudice and degrading the occupation even further for any group involved. "Blacks . . . became associated with servitude generally [and] this association proved disastrous in the nineteenth century, for wherever Blacks served, domestic service was labeled 'nigger's work.'"[105] The distance between master and servant in the South grew; the status of domestic servitude lowered. The treatment of these black servants, combining elements of feudalistic paternalism with the brutalities of chattel slavery, reflected what was perhaps the most anachronistic labor relationship that has existed in this country. Emancipation caused domestic slaves to become low-wage servants and gave them geographical mobility, but the composition of the servant class, the uniquely high ratio of servants to overall population, and the quality of the relationship between employer and employee changed little in the South until World War I.

Not so, however, outside the South. From the mid-nineteenth century until World War I, non-Southern servitude went through a third, very distinct phase: immigrants replaced native-born whites as the dominant group of servants, and employers, as a result, "consciously attempted to enforce social distance between themselves and their servants."[106] Irish and German immigrants were settling in the Northeast, Scandinavians in the Midwest, and Chinese in the Far West.[107] (In the Southwest, Mexican and Indian servants continued to predominate.[108]) All immigrant servants were considered inferior to native white Americans, but the Irish were particularly despised as "vulgar," "childlike," "barbaric," "ignorant," "unclean," and, worst of all, not Christian.[109] As with blacks in the South, class prejudice, ethnic prejudice, and the degradation of menial labor interplayed to reinforce anti-Irish and anti-servitude sentiments: "The Irish seemed more lower-class because they were in domestic labor, and the work itself seemed more menial because the Irish dominated it." The attitude toward and experience of Irish servants is particularly relevant for this study because of Boston's traditionally large Irish servant population. In 1850, for example, 70 percent of the domestics in Boston had been born in Ireland.[110]

Servants' "differentness," then, was interpreted as inferiority, and employers instituted various symbols and forms of behavior designed to increase distance. The term "servant" was reintroduced; various kinds of livery became popular; forms of deference became more formalized;[111] and, undoubtedly the most expensive change, houses were designed with extra accoutrements to keep servants separate (unnecessary servants' entrances, backstairs leading up to servants' attic rooms, kitchens separated from the main rooms by servants' pantries, et cetera).[112]

It is during this third phase that American domestic service, outside the South, exhibited some commonalities with western European patterns—and for the same basic reasons: the second half of the nineteenth century witnessed rapid industrialization and urbanization in this country. As in Europe, the absolute number of domestic servants and the number in proportion to the overall population increased continually during the nineteenth century, with accelerated growth rates during the 1870's and 1880's. (Interestingly, during these decades, there was also a rebirth of the previously abating desire for male servants, suggesting the importance of the status-symbol function of servants to the new wealth of this period.[113])

And, not surprisingly, the occupation became more concentrated in the cities.

The quality of the master-servant relationship, too, came to share similarities with that of western Europe. The expanding American middle and upper classes employed more servants than ever before. This newness to the position combined with the "differentness" of the servants to create a cleavage hitherto far less deep. The appearance of housewives' manuals, training schools for domestics, and regular articles on the subject in popular magazines indicate that in the urban United States, as in Europe, domestic servants were not only ubiquitous but also of great concern. But the lack of the feudal tradition and the democratic undercurrent in American thought continued to distinguish servitude in the United States from that of Europe and continued the philosophical tension that had always existed.[114]

By the end of the nineteenth century, these tensions had begun to manifest themselves among domestics in their accelerated turnover rate, in the flight from service of those capable or "eligible" for factory jobs, and in the beginning of a move from the live-in to the live-out pattern.[115] Simultaneously, technological improvements such as electricity, washing machines, vacuum cleaners, modern plumbing, and gas stoves made servants less necessary. And whether in reaction to servants' discontent or expressing a genuine wish for privacy and self-reliance or both, middle- and upper-income families made changes that facilitated their surviving with less servant help: apartment buildings became popular, doing one's own housework became respectable, and less formal social gatherings became the norm. And in the early twentieth century, many household activities were commercialized in bakeries, dairies, food-processing factories, and garment factories.[116] The essential elements—material and philosophical—of a very fundamental change in American domestic service were developing. But it took World War I to reverse the patterns of the nineteenth century.

The War made more non-servant positions available to both men and women than ever before. Men entered the military or factories; women went into factories and offices in record numbers. Even related occupations, such as office cleaning or working in commercial laundries, expanded and attracted women away from the more stigmatized personal servant position. Almost as important as the new availability of alternative occupations was "the revolution in American manners, morals, and customs that took place in the second decade of the twentieth century."[117] Morals and manners became less rigid; personal freedom, individualism, and self-expression became more highly valued. The position of domestic servant—always of low prestige and affording the least personal freedom of any occupation—was inconsistent with the spirit of the period. It is not surprising, then, that those who could, left. As we have seen, those who could were mainly native-born whites.[118]

By the 1920's, the composition and work patterns of the domestic servant sector had changed: the worker was more likely to be black, older, married, and living out.[119] The migration of blacks north during World War I and the drop in immigration of those foreign-born groups more likely to enter domestic service[120] caused black women to become more significant in the occupation outside the South during and after the 1920's. (Whereas blacks comprised 28.8 percent of all domestics in 1890, they comprised 45.8 percent by 1920—82 percent of all Southern servants, 18 percent of Northern servants, and 9 percent of those in the Western states.[121]) And their increasing presence is part of what stimulated the change to live-out work. Black women were less likely to be able to use the occupation as a stepping stone to other jobs or as a temporary position to be abandoned when they married. And there is evidence that employers in both the North and South preferred black domestics to live at a greater distance than white domestics. For these reasons, in addition to the lessening dependency on servants and the shortening of hours in all occupations, live-out "day work" was becoming more prevalent among all domestics.

This fourth phase in American domestic service deserves particular note for dramatically illustrating the existence of two distinct functions of domestic servitude in modern times. The first is exemplified in industrializing Europe and the United States. The typical female domestic is a young migrant from a poor, non-urban area who engages in live-in domestic service until marriage or a more desirable employment opportunity presents itself. The "career" female domestic is atypical and eventually becomes high in the servant hierarchy, and domestic service functions to absorb and acculturate the large numbers of rural migrants. But in India, South Africa, and the United States, another pattern can be observed: a racially or ethnically subordinate group is "ghettoized" into the occupation.[122] The distinct pattern of domestic service in twentieth-century America—older, married, live-out domestics who retain a lifelong "maid-of-all-work" status and whose daughters may well enter domestic work—appears to be directly related to racism, not only through the exclusion of these women from other jobs, but also by the prevention of men of color from obtaining wages sufficient to support their families. Domestic service, in this context, rather than functioning as a gateway through which socioeconomic marginals pass into the mainstream, functions to reinforce racial and ethnic stereotypes and maintain those biologically "deviant" in a social and economic underclass.[123]

In the twentieth century, the domestic service sector has consistently become smaller in relation to the size of the overall population, the female labor force, and the total number of American families. Its absolute numbers increased (except for a dip during World War I) until World

War II, but government figures indicate a sharp and steady decline after that. In 1900, there were approximately one-and-a-half million domestics; in 1940, the number peaked at 2,277,000; by 1970, the total was back to one-and-a-half million; and in 1979, there were 1,062,000. But whereas the one-and-a-half million of 1900 was 28.7 percent of the female labor force, the similar number of domestics in 1970 represented only 5.1 percent of all female workers.[124]

There are recent developments in domestic service in the United States that are relevant to this study. The 1970 census was the first time this category of work did not contain the largest segment of the black female labor force. In 1940, almost 60 percent of employed black women were domestics; by 1970, only 18 percent were domestics (surpassed by the 26.9 percent in the "other service worker" and the 19.7 percent in the "clerical" categories).[125] Additionally, the exodus of black women from the occupation is currently at a higher rate than that of white women: while 38 percent of all domestics were black in 1970, only 32 percent were in 1979.[126]

Though these census figures reflect real trends, their accuracy and meaning must be tempered by the following considerations. Underreporting in "private household work" has always been widespread and for some groups of workers it may be increasing. The living-out and day-work arrangements facilitate the hiding of work and income. And both employers and domestics have more motivation now than in the past to do so. Social Security legislation included most forms of domestic work in 1951; employers and domestics both avoid paying 5.85 percent of domestics' wages that would be their share of the tax. Minimum wage legislation started covering most forms of domestic work in 1974; in those situations in which the minimum wage is not being paid—most prevalent in the South and in situations involving immigrant workers—there is that additional reason to avoid federal scrutiny.

And, indeed, immigrant women are again increasing in this occupation. Numbers are difficult to estimate both because of the non-reporting and because many of these women, mainly from the Caribbean and Latin America, are lost in the "black" and "hispanic" census categories. But two things are certain about this newest population in American domestic service: because of their precarious material and sometimes legal status, they are the most exploitable group within the domestic servant sector; and because they are Third World women, they will be vulnerable to the "occupational ghettoization" European immigrant women of the nineteenth century escaped.

Another way in which the census figures indicating a decrease in domestics and especially black domestics are misleading is the occupational categorization itself. For within the "other service worker" category are "homemaker/health aides," an occupation I consider disguised domestic work. Homemaker/health aides work for private and public agencies that, through public contracts, place women in the homes of publicly assisted persons (the disabled, aged, handicapped, recuperating, et cetera). The main distinction of this work is that the homemaker works for an agency, not for the individual for whom she is cleaning. The attraction for the worker is that she can usually get placements near her own home and the job does not have the stigma of domestic work. But the work itself is basically similar and the compensation (in the Boston area, at least) is even less than for independent domestic work. No group of homemakers in the Boston area was unionized at the time of my study; none received health insurance, paid vacations, or retirement benefits. The largest homemaker agency in Boston, employing approximately four hundred people, paid from $3.50 to $5.00 an hour. According to the director of this agency, 96 percent of his employees were women and most were "minorities, . . . blacks, Puerto Ricans, Cape Verdeans, West Indians."

Homemaker/health aide agencies proliferated, not surprisingly, with the expansion of social service benefits and the increase in deinstitutionalization of the 1960's.

Another new element in housework since World War II has been the development of commercial cleaning services. Entrepreneurs send teams of workers and sophisticated machinery into homes and specialize in quick, thorough, "heavy" cleaning. It may be assumed that if the numbers of women doing domestic work continues to decrease, such companies will proliferate. However, if the negative attitude toward them of the employers I interviewed for this study reflects a norm, there is no danger of their displacing individual workers.

And not to be overlooked are recent efforts to organize domestic workers. There have been a few small, local efforts (like the United Domestic Workers Organization begun in San Diego by Cesar Chavez), but these have suffered because of limited involvement of domestics themselves. The only national organization, the National Committee on Household Employment (NCHE), encouraged by the Women's Bureau, funded by the Ford Foundation, and housed in the National Urban League offices in New York, played a critical role in having housework covered by minimum-wage legislation in 1974 and has enjoyed moderate success in using the media to publicize issues of concern to houseworkers. However, its efforts to establish local, active chapters have been less than effective. By far most of the domestics in the United States, as in my study, are not part of any such organization.[127]

This survey of domestic service throughout history reveals a picture of a chameleon-like occupation, changing its size, role, and composition in relation to changes in the larger political and economic spheres of the society. But, grounded in stratification, it was always low in the class hierarchy, always composed of people considered inferior (by virtue of their unfree status, their gender, their geographic origins, their lower-class backgrounds, and/or their caste, race, or ethnicity), and always held in the lowest esteem by the overall society, including the domestics themselves. The fact that domestic service is one of the two forms of work historically accepted as "women's work" (the other being prostitution), that it has an ancient and modern association with slavery and is manual and dirtying, makes this occupation one universally despised and those who do it universally dehumanized.

The pattern of the numbers in the domestic service sector burgeoning during the transitional stage of industrialization has been repeated throughout the world, as has the tendency toward urbanization and, to varying degrees, feminization of the occupation. Continuing trends set in the nineteenth century, domestic service in the United States today is typically a female-female relationship made up of a white, middle-class employer and a migrant Third World employee. But before examining more closely the women and the relationship between them, let us look at domestic work itself—its effects and advantages, its conditions and compensations.

3. The Work

The Labor

> Northern employers have a week's work cut out for you for a day or half a day. They pay you good but nine times out of ten you've got to take that money and go to the doctor with it.

Cleaning is indeed hard on the body. The older domestics I interviewed[1] had various physical ailments associated with their work: lower back problems, varicose veins, and, most common, ankle and foot problems. Two had switched to childcare and cooking because they were less tiring. In the early part of this century, black women frequently became laundresses and, according to the three women in my study who had done such work, this was the most physically demanding task of all. Washing machines may have replaced laundresses and other technology may have shortened and lightened other household tasks, but scrubbing floors, ironing, vacuuming with often outdated and heavy machines, and cleaning out closets for four to eight hours at a time remain exhausting work. When riding the trolley and bus home from my domestic jobs, I saw other domestics—usually older women—with a profound and sad, hollow-eyed weariness on their faces, often fighting sleep, ankles swollen, having lost the energy and sociability of the morning's ride to work. My own exhaustion debilitated me for a period of time every evening I worked a full day. And although it may be justly claimed that my previous academic life had hardly prepared me for any kind of all-day physical labor, my reaction was not at all unique. Forty-four-year-old Julia Henry explained why she stopped working for a family in Brookline after three months:

> It was too much work from the beginning. It was two days' work in one. I was washing clothes, ironing. Then I had to do two bathrooms, three bedrooms, vacuum. I'd be so tired. I'd come home. I couldn't go anywhere except to bed. It really wasn't worth it. I told her I couldn't do it all in one day. I finally left.

Esther Jones describes the woman she has worked for for eighteen years:

> She's a driver. Seems like that's where she gets her therapy from—working you. She likes to *work you*. Seems like the harder she works you the better she feels. She just keeps giving you more and more work, telling you

> what to do and how to do it. That's the reason today I require a lot of rest.
>
> When she interviewed me she told me I'd get a two-hour rest every afternoon. But once I started working, she tried to stop me from doing that by telling me to do things. She just likes to see you work!

Four years earlier, Ms. Jones had to have an operation on her ankle. When her doctor advised her against returning to domestic work, this employer suggested she go on welfare. Unwilling to do that, Ms. Jones returned to the same employer, now working full-time, live-out, rather than live-in as before the operation.

Other domestics and a few employers also said that employers liked to see domestics working. Employer Margaret Slater described her displeasure at her worker's inactivity this way: "She really was very good. The only thing that annoyed me was when I would come home and find her sitting down. She'd be just playing with the kids or something. All the cleaning would be finished but it still bothered me to see her sitting." Retired domestic Anne Ryder remembered a time in the 1940's in Cambridge when she was so exhausted she lay on the kitchen floor in the middle of the day. When her employer came in, Ms. Ryder said, "'I'm tired and if you say one word to me I'm going to get up and go home.' 'Oh,' [the employer] said, 'you rest yourself and come and get something to drink.' But, you know, as soon as I had that drink, she had something else for me to do." And May Lund, talking about one of her early day-work experiences in the 1960's, described a pattern I repeatedly encountered in my domestic work:

> The ad stated, "light housekeeping." When I went there she said, "Oh, just take the damp mop and run over the kitchen floor and make the beds and dust and this, that

> and the other." When I got finished, I said, "Oh, wow, this is not bad. I like this!" And then I go back the next week: "When you dust the furniture, put a little polish on that too." Then you go back the next week and: "Oh, would you just throw the clothes in the washer and dryer?" And every week you go back, they're adding more and more and more. And then it was a struggle, I mean it was a *job*, a *race* to get everything done in that eight hours. Every time you go there, there's something else added.

Few of the employers I interviewed mentioned the physical demands of the work. Fifty-five-year-old Frances Stewart related this story about a young Jamaican woman she had imported to be a live-in servant in Chestnut Hill:

> Oh, a funny thing. I thought she must be very homesick. She'd brought up rum and we noticed she was using a *lot* of rum. We wondered if she had a drinking problem. But it turned out she was rubbing her muscles with it [laughter] so they wouldn't tire so much.

And sixty-eight-year-old Marna Houston, who has always done most of her own housework herself, employing help only when her children were small and recently since she's been ill, expresses her understanding of the amount of work involved both in the salary she pays (ten dollars an hour to an Italian-American woman) and in these statements:

> Well, the good thing about it is the independence. One can change jobs easily; you're not tied down by benefits. But the bad part is the labor itself. It can be *hard* physical labor. And, sometimes, there's no gratitude and very poor pay. I think the low prestige of the job is because of

the low pay and menial nature of the work. It's really too bad.

Of my ten employers, only one—a Greek-American woman from a working-class background—was what I considered reasonable and realistic in her expectations. The others, to varying degrees, always demanded more than any one person could accomplish in the given time. At first I actually tried to do everything and would feel frustration as well as exhaustion at my failure; in time I realized that their being overdemanding was the norm and paced myself more wisely. One employer fired me for not working fast enough; the others seemed to expect that I would not complete everything they had asked be done. But seeing me breathing hard, perspiring, and visibly weary never prompted any employer to suggest I take a break—not even when I worked an eight-hour day (with a half-hour for lunch). And this apparently is typical: none of the domestics I talked with took breaks in addition to their lunch. Those working only four or five hours in one house did not stop at all. After a while, I began taking ten-minute breaks in the morning and afternoon on my eight-hour days—incurring reactions ranging from approval to pointed glares. On one occasion, when I sat down to eat an apple after working particularly hard from 9:00 A.M. to 12:30 P.M., the husband of my employer made his disapproval clear. My field notes read as follows:

> It was 12:30 and I, weary and hungry, decided to take a short break and have lunch later. Since he [a fifty-five-year-old psychiatrist] was on the phone in the kitchen, I sat in the dining area, ate an apple I had brought and read a magazine. He could hear me but not see me. As soon as he got off the phone, he walked a roundabout route to go upstairs, apparently so he could see what I was doing.

> Walking by slowly, he literally glared at me. I smiled slightly; he did not return the smile, seeming to want to make it clear he was checking me out and disapproved of my not working. He glared, said nothing, continued upstairs. I resumed work after about ten minutes.

But the reader should be reminded that my taking breaks was entirely out of the ordinary for this occupation; the morning and afternoon breaks other blue-collar workers take for granted are practically unknown in household work.

Like former domestic Elizabeth Roy, whose quote opens this section on work, many of the women who had worked in both the North and South commented that Northern employers worked domestics harder. They attributed it to Northerners' being less caring and paying more. When most forms of private household work were included in minimum-wage legislation (1974), Northern employers reacted by raising the salaries to at least the legal minimum but cutting back hours. (The day-work salaries of the 1960's, according to the domestic interviewees, ranged from 60¢ to $1.65 an hour in the Boston area.) While decreasing hours, however, employers did not decrease the amount of work they wanted done. And the crunch was on. Elizabeth Roy explains it this way:

> Any time you do "day work," you make more than a regular five days a week in one place—because some of the people will want you to do a whole week's work in one day! You make more money but it's not worth it. You really have to break your neck.

> You'd be surprised at the mess some of these people leave. It's really bad. I went out to Newton one day and I tell you! She wanted the *whole house* cleaned in one day.

> And it was awful—dust you could sprout any kind of seeds in! She wanted the windows, the blinds, everything done. I told her I'd do what I could.
>
> She didn't want me to come back after I put the price to her: $35 for the day. [That's the price she'd been told on the phone] but she probably thought I'd do it for less. They con some of our people with old clothes and stuff. And the people coming from the [West Indian] Islands, they're really being exploited!

Note that Ms. Roy, a former vulnerable and exploited migrant from the South who has since become a matron in a state-run women's shelter, is conscious of the fact that today it is foreign-born Third World women who are "really being exploited." And domestic May Lund describes the change to partial days similarly:

> You see, what happened was, the people cut down the hours. They generally don't want you more than four or five hours a day. Only one lady I worked for eight hours a day. Just one lady. The people cannot afford to pay you. . . . Even though, back then, you worked eight hours and got ten dollars—they got the whole house cleaned.

Another element of domestic service that too often adds to the physical demands of the work is the poor quality of the equipment supplied by the employers. I found this statement by May Lund to be true in over half of the houses in which I worked: "Some of the equipment you work with, you don't know if it will make it from one cleaning to the next." Dilapidated, outdated, or very cheap equipment forces the worker to compensate for its ineffectiveness with extra physical effort. In a split-level ranch house in

Needham, I was asked to scour kitchen counter tops, stove, and sink using only bar soap and cotton rags. In a luxurious house in Wayland, filled with original Picassos, Braques, and Chagalls, I was given a cheap five-and-ten-cents-store mop and pail to clean a particularly dirty kitchen floor. And in a modest but comfortable three-story home in Newton, where I worked along with a domestic who had been there fifteen years, we had to vacuum with a twenty-five to thirty pound cleaner that had been there even longer. One wonders how long the employing women would retain such equipment if they themselves had to use it.

Hours

Intense and exhausting work is more characteristic of day work than of live-in or full-time live-out work. But the trade-off is in hours and pay. Ten- and twelve-hour work days are not, as one might assume, a thing of the distant past, particularly not for live-in domestics. In 1964, seventeen-year-old Edith Lincoln was brought to Milton by a couple who had met her during their vacation on the Cape. Though they had no children, Ms. Lincoln left after four months because she considered the work and hours excessive.

> I worked from the time I got up 'till the time I went to bed. I said, "This is not for me!" It was a big house. I had my own apartment on the third floor. When you work for older people, they like everything done just so. You got your floors, you got the walls, the windows. . . . During the day, it's a lot.

Asha Bell lived in for three years in the early 1970's in Chestnut Hill:

> I had to see after the baby, make the beds, keep the house clean, things like that. I was free after the kids went to bed, about 7:30 or 8:00 unless the [employers] went out. Then I had to listen out for the kids until they came home. I started about 7:30 in the morning, but in the afternoon after lunch, I had a rest period. It was when the baby took her nap that I had a rest for about an hour, hour and a half. And I had Sundays and Thursdays off.

For this fifty- to seventy-hour week, Ms. Bell was paid seventy dollars.

Marva Woods lived with a family with two children in Chestnut Hill for eleven years from the mid-1960's to the mid-1970's. The family had brought her up from South Carolina:

> I just worked until I got the children to bed. Every Thursday and every other Sunday was off. I got up in the morning, fixed breakfast, got the children ready for school, and carried little John to nursery school. I'd get them all off then start doing my housework: the washing, cleaning up. John would come home about twelve. I'd go and get him and give him his lunch and put him to bed. I would iron or something while he was in bed. When he got up, I'd take him for a walk. Then I'd cook dinner and serve it. After I cleaned up the kitchen and got the children to bed, I was finished. . . . She started me off at thirty-seven dollars a week, then she gave me a raise and I was making fifty-five dollars.

It is not coincidental that at the time of these experiences, all of these women were recent arrivals to Boston or were recruited from their homes specifically for these jobs. Margo Townsend, who directed a local black women's club's program for domestics in the late 1960's and early 1970's, and who, as part of her job, regularly talked to employers, explains their preference for such women this way:

> At one time, they would stipulate, "I want a Southern girl." They like the "Yes, Ma'am" and the "Yes, Sir." They *loved* that. But, later on, they'd say "I want a West Indian girl." Now the reason for that was when they got on that job, they'd do anything, they'd work any number of hours—because here's an opportunity to come to this country. And they would work for less money. So everybody wanted a West Indian. No one ever asked for a Northern girl. They felt they'd get more loyalties from people from other places.

And the director of a Newton employment agency that places domestics in both live-in and live-out positions confirmed this view:

> Right now I'm getting a lot of calls from people who have heard about the boat people—the people from Vietnam, Cambodia, Haiti, Cuba, and anybody that's coming in—Chinese people. The living over there and the living here—they don't understand what's going on. They'll do anything. I just had one woman come in who requested a Cambodian or Vietnamese. Why? Because she can get them cheap!

The Pay

But what is the pay really like? From the point of view of domestics, it is "fair," "much better than years ago," "better for whites than for blacks," "slave wages," "OK now," et cetera. Domestics' attitudes toward it range as widely as the pay scale itself. I encountered situations of live-out workers making from $3.50 to $10.00 an hour (though the highest salary I found for a black worker was $8.00 an hour).[2] I heard of employers paying the foreign-born below the minimum wage but never encountered this situation first hand. And recall that before 1974, domestics in Boston were making from 60¢ to $1.65 an hour. My impression, from my own job hunts and from my discussions with employers and domestics, is that since 1974 most Boston employers have paid live-out help above the minimum wage.

Employers' attitudes toward the pay also varied widely. A few, like Elsa Coleman, demonstrated compassion and sensitivity to the low rewards of this occupation: "I think they work awfully hard and don't get a tremendous salary for the amount of work they do. There's such insecurity that goes along with not making a lot of money. I have a sense of their barely making it; it's a hand-to-mouth existence." Many more were like Alice Lynch, expressing little interest in the topic. Having had cleaners and childcare workers for over thirty years, Ms. Lynch has never given paid vacation or deducted for Social Security. When asked if she thought wages had been fair, she responded indifferently: "They probably haven't been, but I just paid the prevailing wage."

Other employers rationalized the low wages they had paid (particularly before 1974) by suggesting the workers did not care about their lack of money. Jocelyn Minor, for example, has always paid at the lower end of the wage scale. Talking about a former employee, she justified her wages in this way: "Well, I drove her home a couple of times and she lived in this dreadful hotel-type place in Newton. But she liked it! So I think the pay was fair in view of that. I never thought about it really." Frances Stewart displayed similar thoughtlessness when talking about a black domestic she had brought from Alabama through an agency. The woman had come to Boston to work and support three children in Alabama whom she eventually was able to bring up. Yet speaking of the forty dollars a week she was paying (in the early 1960's), Ms. Stewart said, "She never cared much about not having money. It never bothered her." Ava Pearson justified the wages to her fifteen-year Irish domestic (wages she was unable to remember) in a similar fashion: "She has a very positive attitude. She's always been poor. Her husband was a hod carrier. I don't know that the lack of material things were that important in her life." And a few of the older employers were openly resentful about the federally mandated increase in pay. This Chestnut Hill school teacher was the most explicit:

> I used to have a woman for a full day. But now they charge so much! We have to just make do. . . . Domestics make too much money now. You know, I'm a teacher and I don't make as much an hour as some domestics do. It's gotten all out of hand. . . . It's unskilled labor; you don't need any training for it. Maybe there was a time when domestics weren't paid enough but now it's gotten to the opposite extreme. Do you think that that's right? That an unskilled worker should make more than a teacher? . . . I remember when I was paying twenty-four dollars a week! And my mother had a full-time woman for six dollars a week!

Live-in pay is more difficult to measure because room and board are given free and because of the ill-defined hours of work. The director of a Newton employment agency exclusively for domestics, whom I interviewed as a researcher, told me live-in pay ranged from $175 to $300 a week. The director of another Newton agency, to whom I talked as a job applicant, said the range was from $125 to

$200. And the head of the newly formed domestics section of a large downtown Boston employment agency told me (as a researcher) that live-in positions were paying from $100 to $175. Since none of the domestics or employers I interviewed were currently involved in live-in situations, my information on this is limited to these figures supplied by employment agency personnel. The rather large discrepancies between them may be accounted for by their serving different employing clienteles and/or their wish to inflate their figures to attract or impress me.

From the interviews with domestics and employers came the fact that a wage hierarchy within the occupation indeed exists. The domestics I interviewed confirmed my impression that the further out one works from central Boston, the higher the pay. May Lund said:

> When you don't have transportation, you have to get on the busline. You had to keep in mind what a convenient location was, as far as transportation. Blacks end up working in Brookline, Chestnut Hill, Newton because most of them don't have cars and those are the areas convenient to get to. But I drive and the further out you go, the more money you get. . . . They know they have to pay for the distance. They know no one's going out that far for nothing. The best you can get in Brookline is five-fifty. And I'm getting eight dollars in Wayland.

Comments by other domestics, however, indicated they felt the wage differences were based on race. For example, Nancy Clay, a domestic for over twenty-five years now making five dollars an hour, asked me what was the highest salary I had heard of a day worker making. At the time it was eight dollars an hour. Her response was: "Oh, yes, but if they're willing to pay that much, they'll only give it to a white domestic."

It is a fact that the areas of Boston in which most black domestics live—Roxbury, Dorchester, and Mattapan—connect most conveniently on public transportation with those areas that appear to pay the lowest—Brookline, Chestnut Hill, and Newton. But do these areas pay the lowest because the people in them know they have access to a large labor pool or because there is a deliberate design to pay black women less? In any case, a wage hierarchy does exist in domestic service in the Boston area and, whether because of racism, geography, or poverty (not owning a car), black women are on the bottom of it.

Though domestics varied in their attitudes toward current wages, they were unanimous in their complaints about the lack of benefits in this occupation. Dorothy Aron's remarks were typical: "The worst thing about domestic work is that there are no benefits, no sense of security. You're not covered for any unforeseen emergency. You're not even covered for tomorrow: they'll go away in a minute and leave you stuck." No domestic worker I talked with nor any past or present employee of the employers I interviewed had any form of medical coverage through their jobs. None had sick leave; if they were unable to make it to work, they forfeited their pay. Nine of the eleven women still active in domestic work received paid vacations ranging from one to two weeks. As the above quote indicates, day workers are particularly vulnerable to employers' out-of-town trips; whether for two days or two months, no day worker was paid for the period employers were away. And although all of the situations in my study were covered by the Social Security law, only eight domestics had Social Security taken out and two of the employers interviewed were taking it out.[3] None of my ten employers mentioned Social Security. Clearly, in domestic service, non-compliance with Social Security legislation is rampant.

The reasons for such widespread disregard for the Social Security laws are numerous. The employer would have to do additional paperwork and contribute 5.85 percent of the employee's wages as her share of the Social Security tax. Many domestics, too, prefer not to have Social Security withheld: the typical hand-to-mouth existence of low-wage workers makes immediate cash more important than protection for the future. Employer Karen Edwards would prefer to take out Social Security but "I have never found anyone who would let me take it out. I would always offer. My husband is a lawyer and likes to be honest; it makes him feel good. And I believe it's right; it's really best for people." A few employers expressed ignorance that the Social Security law covered their employees. Frances Stewart, for example, maintained: "No, I've never taken out Social Security or given her a paid vacation. You have no such responsibility to day workers, to my knowledge." But Holly Woodward's deliberate neglect is more typical: "No, I never took out Social Security. We rationalized it. Nobody did it; why should you be a dope and add to your burdens?"

The two women who did take out Social Security, Ava Pearson and Elsa Coleman, both stated that they did so at their husbands' insistence:

> I always took out Social Security. My husband is very firm on this. He's a financial officer in a corporation. He's conscious of the law and basically I think it's the best thing. This sometimes presents a problem. . . . Some help is not willing to do this. (Ms. Pearson)

> We have gotten into discussions with the last few people. My husband and I feel very strongly that we have to pay employee taxes on the money that we pay domestic help—because that is legal, what we're supposed to

do. . . . We do it because it's illegal not to and because my husband wants the childcare deduction on his taxes. (Ms. Coleman)

The prevalence of disregard for the law and the comfort expressed with that disregard by both domestics and employers suggests that the women may see domestic work as exceptional, not quite as legitimate a job as others, not to be taken entirely seriously as an employer-employee relationship. Pamela Kane comes close to saying this: "No, I've never taken out for Social Security or made arrangements about sick pay or vacation. In this kind of job, there is no formalized arrangement. I can't imagine what the [vacation arrangement] would be, but certainly time without pay." The isolation of the relationship undoubtedly facilitates this attitude. But the historical basis of the occupation—in slavery and feudalism where the servant was owned or considered a part of the household—may also explain the personal, extra-legal approach most women take toward this labor arrangement.

A part of that slavery/feudalistic type of domestic service was the protective obligations of the master or mistress. While many possible forms of protection, like health insurance or retirement pensions, do not exist, one form, the giving of gifts, is a still flourishing carryover of that tradition. Employers reported having given all kinds of items—beds, tables, refrigerators, leftover food—but, most commonly, they gave old clothes. By far, most of the employers who had given such gifts (and this included all of the women over forty-five) were entirely comfortable with, even proud of, having done so. (Only two employers expressed reservations because they had detected resentment in their domestics.[4]) Domestics reported having been given such items in the North and in the South, in the 1980's as much as in earlier decades. Domestics said they always accepted anything offered and acted grateful. This was what was expected of them; this was "part of the job." A full analysis of why this custom has persisted in this occupation throughout history will be undertaken in Chapter 5. At this point, what is important is that this form of "payment in kind" is an extremely common practice in this occupation and can be considered one of the material compensations of domestic service.

Other Aspects of the Work

Four other aspects of the work that came up in my interviews with employers and domestics are worthy of mention: the aloneness of the job, the monotony of the work, the immediate gratification of the payment system, and the sense of accomplishment physical labor yields. Though some of the older domestics had been part of servant staffs in Boston (frequently along with Irish women), all of the interviewees had worked alone in the last few decades. But attitudes toward this varied dramatically: many of the day workers considered the "independence" and "autonomy" one of the most positive aspects of the job, all of those who had lived in identified loneliness as one of the more difficult aspects of their positions.

During her years doing day work, May Lund has developed a style of only working for women who are out of the house all day: "I like working with things. They have no feelings; you have no ties. . . . I like houses. I don't have to like people. . . . No aggravation. You're your own boss. You do what you want to do. You put your money in your pocket and you come home."

Mary Dixon, too, prefers cleaning houses when no one is at home: "I like to do housework. But I don't have that much patience with people. I'd rather no one be around and just let me do my work. It feels independent. No one to have to talk to, to bother you. I work much better when there's no one around." When I asked Pat Owens why she liked housework as an occupation, she answered quickly and energetically:

> The best thing about domestic work is that you're your own boss. . . . I didn't like factory work. I don't like a group of people, a bunch of women. I don't like tattle-tale people. I *love* to get up in the morning and know I have a job to go on. And know when I get there, I'm my own boss. I have nobody standing over me. Nobody telling me what to do because I know what my job is.

Is it ever lonely?

> No! With televisions, why, how could it be lonely? You've got a TV in every room and a radio in every room. How could you be lonely?

And Elizabeth Roy also considers this one of the more positive aspects of domestic work: "You're free to be your own boss. I can do my work more professionally being by myself. Someone over me makes me nervous."

But there were day workers who did not like the isolated aspect of their work. Dorothy Aron had done factory work before becoming a domestic: "I like working around other people. It's more social. This kind of work gets lonely sometimes. Nobody sees you. . . . You don't make any new friends at this kind of work. It can be lonely." And Julia Henry, forced into domestic work because of physical disabilities that stopped her from typing, also finds the loneliness problematic:

> Look at my weight. You know, I would never get this big working in a laundry 'cause you move around so much more. And in the laundry and with typing, you're with the public. When you're in people's houses, nobody sees you so you don't care. And you just eat more too. You

> bring your lunch and you snack 'cause you're bored. I prefer more public kinds of jobs. Domestic work is so lonely. I bring a radio sometimes but it doesn't help much.

All of those who had lived in mentioned the loneliness of that kind of experience, most keenly felt, as one might expect, when the worker was new to Boston. Esther Jones, Asha Bell, and Joan Fox were three of the domestics who identified this as one of the psychologically difficult aspects of the job:

> Usually sleeping in was all right. Except in the springtime. Oh, my goodness, the springtime. I would get spring fever. Want to get out and see people. I would hate myself for sleeping in. (Ms. Jones)

> Yes, it was lonely when I first came to Cambridge. They paid me OK. And the laundress and cleaner were nice to me. Mary was the cook. But I only knew two people in Boston then. And it would be very lonely sometimes. (Ms. Bell)

> It was real hard for me when I first came [from South Carolina]. It was so different here. It was cold. The people was cold. I didn't know anyone outside the house [in Newton] and it's not easy to make friends when you're living in. (Ms. Fox)

A few employers were conscious of the loneliness of their live-in help. Frances Stewart, for example, said: "The live-in help usually had problems with loneliness and culture shock. Well, of course—they were from very different kinds of places. I remember one of the Jamaican girls just curling up on the couch, looking into space. She was depressed."

For the non-English-speaking domestic, of course, the isolation is even more intense. Although beyond the scope of this study, my interview with a Costa Rican domestic, who came to Boston speaking no English and lived with a family in Wellesley that spoke no Spanish, gives us a glimpse of this experience:

> I did everything, cooking, cleaning, everything. I usually worked from seven A.M. to seven P.M. . . . I had Sundays and Tuesdays off. But I didn't know anyone who spoke Spanish and it was hard to get around. I would just go shopping and then go home. I was very homesick and lonely. There was no one I could even talk to.

The combination of adjusting to a new culture and climate, working long hours, and not living near any other black people was difficult. Employers sometimes exacerbated the problem by discouraging their employees from going out or deliberately impeding their efforts to make contact with the black community. Margo Townsend, who, as stated, directed a training and support program for domestics from the late 1960's through the early 1970's, knew of such cases:

> Some of the employers felt Thursday and Sunday also belonged to them. "I don't want you doing this and I don't want you doing that. I want you home at this hour." Many domestics who'd been here [in the Boston area] for a number of years told us they'd never heard of our program because their employers never let them come into Boston. Imagine saying someone didn't *let* you come into Boston? With the streetcar right there? The employers would tell them it was dangerous. The domestics would ask where the black area was so they

could find a hairdresser and the employers would just say, "I don't know."

Domestic work, like many other blue- and white-collar jobs, can be repetitious. This note was left for one of the employers I interviewed by her once-a-week cleaning woman:

> Dear Mrs. Peabody,
> I came here to work today. But I started in your bathroom and realized that *if I scrubbed that toilet one more time,* I would flip. I'm sorry to give you such short notice. I won't be back.
> Goodbye.
> (Emphasis mine.)

Some workers said cleaning a house was challenging the first few times but after a while it became monotonous. Though the longest I worked for an employer was only six months, in far less time than that I found familiarity (with the house) bred boredom. May Lund consciously tries to counteract that reality by her approach:

> In order to avoid the work becoming monotonous, I change it up. What I have to do is each time I do one extra thing. A certain amount of things are basic, but I got to do something different each time. When I first started out doing domestic work twenty years, I got annoyed at how people messed up things after I cleaned and I had to go back and do the same thing over and over again. But I put this stuff in perspective and got my head turned around. I knew I was fighting a losing battle.

But Dorothy Aron's attitude is more representative of the women I talked with: "Of course you get tired of washing the same kitchen floor, making the same beds the same way week after week. It *is* more interesting, more of a challenge in the beginning. But the routine is part of the job. That's just part of what domestic work is." Domestics' complaints about the monotony of the work may be the other side of employers' complaints that, over time, domestics do less and less work. Employers Elsa Coleman and Marna Houston were dissatisfied with their servants' cutting hours but did not speak to them about it or fire them.

> Well, at first, she [a white domestic from Watertown] was very good. I was paying her twenty dollars for four hours in the early 1970's and she was very reliable. But then she came less and less time and was not doing a very good job. You see, she really wanted to be an actress. She started doing a really terrible job but I liked her a lot and couldn't bear to fire her. She stayed about a year and a half. Then she called the night before she was supposed to work and said she had a job at Filene's and wouldn't be back. I was real angry because it was on no notice whatsoever. (Ms. Coleman)

> Well, I needed her [an Italian-American domestic], you know. I do think she's too expensive. And she's working less and less for me—at the same price. . . . She used to call me Mrs. Houston but she changed on her own; now she calls me Marna. (Ms. Houston)

Sylvia Peabody, however, was less tolerant:

> We had agreed that she would get fifty dollars for six hours. . . . The first time she stayed the whole six hours but didn't clean the whole house. That was OK because she had said the first few times she would be slower until she got the house into shape and she got used to it. The next time she came I had given her a key, and she got sick

> while she was working. So she left early. She told me later that she had been here three hours and she came back on another day for three hours. And she just didn't clean all that well. So I was a bit concerned about that. The next time she came again while I was working. This time not only did she not clean the whole house but she didn't do a job I had left her a note about. She had said in the beginning she didn't like new assignments popping up but preferred a regular routine. But when I came home, I was really annoyed. And I didn't think she had even stayed the full six hours. I felt I had been more than fair and she was taking advantage. So I called her and explained all that and cancelled our arrangement.

And Holly Woodward, an employer for over twenty-five years, offers an additional insight, beyond the monotony of the work, that might help account for the "pattern" of domestics' doing less over time:

> Then there was a married woman with children, an Irish lady. Over a two-year period, she did less and less and less for the same amount of money. This has been a pattern with the people who have worked for me. I would like to anticipate it by giving them a raise but sometimes that doesn't work.

> For me, maybe I'm projecting, but I think there's just a natural resentment from working in some other woman's house that I think is built into this kind of job. This job is so much more personal; there is so much more capacity to make judgments because you're in such close quarters.

Only one domestic, May Lund, brought up the issue of the immediate gratification of the payment system of domestic work. But it had impressed me as significant during my field work as a domestic. An entry in my field notes at the end of the second week reads as follows:

> The immediate gratification of being paid at the end of the day gives a kind of pleasure that a once-a-week check does not. Is this one of the attractions of domestic work? Also, having cash coming in so regularly seems to give an illusionary sense of more affluence than is actually the case. One is almost never without some money—or knows it will be coming within a day. Does this somehow mitigate against the reality that bills cannot always be paid, that there is never any extra to save?

May Lund's reaction is similar to mine:

> It's a lot of money fast. And that makes you feel good. Domestic work is rewarding because you get immediate gratification. That day, that very day you work, you get paid. What other job gives you that? The problem is, it's not a continuous flow. You can't depend on it.

There was a two-month period during my domestic work when my pay was equivalent to what it had been when I taught one course the previous year at a local college: $270 a month. However, I had received a check once a month from the college and cash daily from the domestic work. The form of payment from domestic work gave me more pleasure and sense of affluence than had the check from the college. I suspect that all Americans are conditioned to have a positive emotional response to green cash that checks, credit, and foreign exchange of equivalent value do not elicit. Receiving regular cash was more pleasurable than receiving an occasional check; it may be assumed that it is pleasurable for other domestics as well.

A few domestics mentioned the sense of accomplishment one could get from domestic work. For Dorothy Aron, one of the attractions of the work is the fact that "there is a beginning and an end. And you know when you've got to that end, and you feel good about getting there." Odette Harris has had the opportunity to compare different types of work:

> When I switched from physical work to mental work, I had to deal with my own self—because I couldn't measure what I did for the day. You know, mentally I was tired, and I seemed to have done a lot of work, but I couldn't measure it like you can measure housework. When you can go back and see the bathroom clean, the kitchen clean, you get that feeling of satisfaction.

And May Lund agrees:

> It was the only kind of job I could go on and see my sense of accomplishment right there. My rewards are there when I finish and close that door. . . . You have to see an end to your job. In domestic work, you get to that end. You get to these four rooms, you get done with the bathroom. You get the whole house back together in order.

These issues were noteworthy but by no means universally expressed. Not every domestic mentioned the monotony of the work nor the sense of accomplishment from it. Not every employer said domestics work less overtime. Only former live-in workers were unanimous on the existence of loneliness, and, as stated, only Ms. Lund brought up the immediate gratification of the payment system. But I consider each of these issues noteworthy to complete the picture (along with the description of the physical demands of the work, the wages and other compensations, hours, and time off) of the overall work conditions of domestic work.

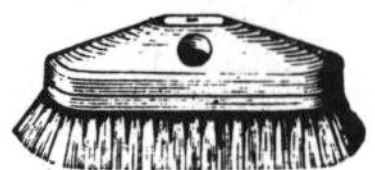

4. The Women

The mistress-servant relationship is one of the more private labor arrangements existing: it takes place within private households between fairly isolated individuals. As multi-servant households become more and more rare, the typical domestic works alone; as the nuclear neolocal family pattern becomes more prevalent, the employer administers the daily chores of her house alone. A sense of isolation surrounds the job and the relationship: there are no co-workers or co-managers on the spot to support, reinforce, compete with, or guide behavior. Consultations with others in similar positions must take place haphazardly during off hours; the job situation is typically one of a single employer dealing with a single employee. For four or forty or sixty hours each week, each woman encounters the other essentially alone; other family members are on the periphery; the intensity of the arrangement is between the women.

What these women are like, how they came to enter into such an arrangement, how they assess the work and one another, and what kinds of circumstances they prefer are the topics to be explored in this chapter. The sources of information are, for the most part, the women; my descriptions and the issues I focus on are guided by the material of my interviews with them (supplemented by my domestic work experience and discussions with other individuals and agency personnel). For that reason, the attempt in this and subsequent chapters is to let the women speak for themselves as much as possible.

While the domestic service relationship is between two individual women, the kind of dynamic they create in the dyad is greatly influenced by the ideas and customs they have inherited from the larger society. The women, indeed, bring originality and creativity to their socially generated roles, but the parameters of the roles are set by forces external to the dyad: the history, traditions, and institutions of the society in which it exists. And the particular tone the women bring to these predetermined roles is as much influenced by their class, ethnic, regional, and racial backgrounds and by the fact that they are women interacting with other women as it is by the traditions around domestic servitude in the United States and in the West.

As we look at the women, it is important never to lose sight of their connectedness to these larger social units. While adults must be held responsible for their ideas and behavior, while we want to see the individuality and freedom of each of these women, we must recognize too the external limitations placed on their life choices by the factors of class, race, and gender. It is a delicate conceptual balance we are forced to maintain if we are to at once see the people as they are and discern the social patterns they reflect and perpetuate.

Becoming an Employer

Who are the employers of domestics and how did they become employers? They may be, of course, of any nationality, race, or class from lower working to upper. Nationally, employers include a broad spectrum of the American population: middle-class Afro-Americans in Washington, D.C., or Atlanta may have employed domestics for generations; old Mexican-American families in the Southwest may still maintain staffs of household workers; middle-income Asians in San Francisco may employ other Asians for housework; bachelors and widowers in all areas may hire women to clean for them; and it is not unusual in the South for blue-collar families to have a servant. But as common as these categories of employers may be in certain locales, nationally they are untypical; most employers have been and are white, middle to upper income, and female. In these ways, my twenty interviewees and ten employers were typical; in some other ways, however, they were not.

The twenty employers I interviewed all lived in the Boston area.[1] They ranged in age from twenty-nine to seventy-six and had employed domestic help from two to forty years. Ten had been born in Massachusetts, six in the New York City area, one in Philadelphia, and three in the Midwest. All were born and raised in urban areas. Their current annual family incomes ranged from $12,000 to over $100,000. The two lowest incomes ($12,000 and $25,000) were of the two widows. Except for them, the lowest income was $40,000 a year. Their educational levels ranged from two years of college (two women) to three Ph.D.'s. Fifteen were either M.A.'s or M.S.W.'s. Nine were

Jewish, two were Irish, and the rest were WASP's. (It is in these latter categories—educational level and ethnicity—that my interviewees cannot be considered representative of all white female employers nationally; though it is impossible to ascertain the national breakdown of employers' educational levels or ethnicity, it is highly improbable that almost 50 percent are Jewish or that 90 percent have a master's degree or better. In these two aspects, my interviewees appear to be untypical. It may be assumed that because of these characteristics they represent the more liberal, more progressive, and better informed end of the white female employers' spectrum.) All of the women had some kind of household help at the time of the interviews (spring 1982). Eleven were working full-time, two were temporarily not working because of new babies, two worked part-time, two were retired, and three had never worked. All of the women, except the two widows, were living with their husbands.

The ten employers for whom I worked represent a broader educational spectrum of the employing sector. Because of the situation, however, I have less data on them. Their ages ranged from thirty-three to seventy and they had had previous domestic help from two to thirty-five years. They were all in the Boston area.[2] Six were Jewish, two Greek, and two WASP's.[3] Their educational levels are partly speculative on my part: two apparently had no college, two had B.A.'s, six had some graduate education, but none of my employers had a Ph.D.

When and how did they come to employ help? The answer to this points to the importance of class background, of tradition, and of modelling. For the employers I interviewed, the single most important element in their decision to enter into this arrangement was the role of their mothers—both as models and as instigators. Typically, they came to define themselves as needing help around the time of the birth of their first child. (The two who had domestic help prior to their first pregnancy were both married and in graduate school at the time.) A few had nurses for a few weeks after the birth; most had cleaning and/or childcare domestics start coming on a permanent basis. Many of the older women had had live-in help because "live-in was a lot less expensive. Day work was maybe ten dollars a day [in the 1950's]. But for forty dollars a week and food, you also had someone to clear the kitchen after dinner and be available most of the time." Fifty-six-year-old Frances Stewart, who has had help for over thirty years, hired her first domestic in 1948:

> We were in a garden apartment. The first person I had was a babysitter. She was Irish. Her mother was a school teacher and she was the youngest of ten kids. She was about fifteen or sixteen. Her grandparents, I think, had come from Ireland. She came three times a week: Tuesdays and Thursdays right from school until after supper and Saturday afternoons. So I did have regular help when my first child was born.
>
> At the same time, I had a cleaning woman who came once a week. After a while, she was replaced by a man, a Newton fireman. On his days off, he would come and clean. Probably undercover, I'm not sure.

Similarly, forty-seven-year-old Carolyn Oxford began hiring when her first child was three months old. She found two sources from which she could get help below the going rate of the early 1960's.

> I got a series of girls to come and live with me from the "Family Plan Helpers" program at the Florence Crittendon Home [for unwed mothers]. I learned about the program from my sister. The problem was, though, that

> the people kept changing. I stopped during my second pregnancy because I thought that situation, my pregnancy, might not be good for the girls. . . .
>
> Then there were a series of girls from Norway. I made arrangements for them to come to the U.S. It was cheaper than hiring Americans: twenty-five dollars a week plus room and board. They usually left to get married. One married but continued to work for me from Monday to Friday. . . .
>
> The duties of all my live-in help was primarily childcare. Housework was secondary.

And sixty-year-old Margaret Slater, who also retained help after the birth of her first child, reveals a secondary function of her "mother's helper":

> My first child was born [in 1955] eleven months after we got married. My husband was finishing up his Ph.D. at Cornell but he was travelling back and forth to Boston a lot. I hired Ann to help me with the baby. She was a black undergraduate at Cornell. She stayed with me during the week and went to her family's house in Ithaca on weekends. Really, I hired her partly to help me take care of the baby and partly because I didn't like being alone so much.

(As will be seen in the upcoming discussion on relationship between employers and servants, domestics' filling companionship needs is not a rare phenomenon.)

None of the women under forty had had live-in help, but the circumstances of their first hiring a domestic were similar. Elsa Coleman, a thirty-five-year-old social worker, is typical:

> The first one was Joan [in 1977]. It was right around the time I had my first child. I was feeling, as I do now, that housework is always the last thing I ever want to do or can get to and that I really needed somebody else to do that for me. I think it was right after my first child was born and I was working half-time. Basically I dislike housework and it's just my last priority. I guess, in my "advancing years," I do like to have the house clean whereas before I could tolerate more mess. She was one day every other week.

Thus, most employers felt the need for help around the time of the birth of their first child. But how did they actually find the worker? In many cases, as stated, the employer's mother played a major role in the process. Some mothers, like Elsa Coleman's, gave money to pay for the help as a gift.

> My second child was born two years ago. And my mother, as a baby present, gave me, as she phrased it, "a month of housecleaning," a person once a week for a month. And I said that I preferred to spread it out over two months and have the person come every other week 'cause I felt that kept the house at a level I was comfortable with. She told me to find the person and tell her how much it was. So I found Jenny—through an ad she had placed in the Watertown paper.

But most mothers took even more active roles. Karen Edwards' mother shared with her daughter some of the time of the woman she had employed full-time for thirteen years: "As soon as I came from the hospital [in 1961], my mother started sending me Agnes for half a day each week. That lasted four years. I didn't pay anything; it was just included in Agnes' regular weekly salary, whatever that was." In the early 1940's, Susan Keplin's mother got help for her daughter in two ways:

> When I became pregnant with my first child, my mother thought that it was very bad that I should not have any help at all. She sent me a woman to do the heavy cleaning once a week. This was her regular woman; she worked for my mother every other day. I think she was paying her around five dollars a day—I don't really remember. She stayed about a year.
>
> Then when I was pregnant with my second child, my mother thought it was *terrible* that I didn't have any help. And so she sent me a woman to live in—but this time I paid for her. I think it was about eighteen dollars a week. My mother found her for me. I remember this very well. She saw this girl standing on the street, an Irish girl, looking at want ads. This was near Coolidge Corner. My mother just walked up to her and asked her if she was looking for a job. And she said yes. So my mother told her she had a job for her and she sent her to me.

It was not only mothers in close proximity who "loaned" their help to their daughters. Holly Woodward's mother sent live-in Constance from Brooklyn, New York, to Boston on three occasions to stay with the Woodwards for the two weeks following the births of their three children. And one of my employers, who was pregnant during the period of my employment, told me her mother in New Jersey was planning to drive her live-in Haitian domestic to Boston to keep house for my employer for three weeks following the birth of her baby.

Though not all of the mothers of my interviewees played such direct roles in hiring help for their daughters, all did play a less direct but more significant role—as models. All of my interviewees' mothers had employed domestic help while my interviewees were growing up. Every employer of domestics had had the opportunity to observe her mother in the role of an employer of domestics. One aspect of the process of identification with the mother's role was revealed in an informal interview with John Green, a young man who had also grown up with live-in help. When describing the situations of the series of women who had cleaned house and taken care of him, he constantly included himself as one of their employers. For example, from the time he was six until he was ten, a woman named Mariam had cooked, cleaned, and taken care of him:

> She was live-in. *We gave her weekends off.* Come to think of it, it was Thursdays and Sundays off. She was largely in charge of taking care of me; more so that, I think, than anything else. But she did some cooking and cleaning. . . . She also played games with me; the only maid I had that ever did that. And she'd watch television with me. And eventually it got to the point apparently that she spent more time with me than she did on her housework. And *we eventually had to get rid of her* for that reason. . . . (Emphasis mine.)

> But she and I became very close. . . . I felt close to her as if she was a friend, a playmate in a sense. And yet someone who had this odd kind of control over me, authority over me. Therefore, I really never came to love her. She was an older person who could have possibly taken the place of a surrogate mother but never quite did.

Why do you think she didn't become a surrogate mother?

> To be frank, I think it was because she was a maid and therefore had a certain stigma attached to her—which I understood even then, in some primitive way. And I understood that she was from a different social [class]. And, of course, she was black and that had to do with it.

The statement suggests that growing up in such a household teaches the child at a very young age not only appropriate behavior toward servants but the profound significance of class and race differences in this country. And it gives the child the opportunity to conceive of him or herself as an employer long before he or she is actually in a position to employ a domestic.

While practical need was the reason most employers gave for initially hiring domestic help, it is clear that because of their childhood experiences and expectations, tradition played as important a role. Some statements of employers address this directly. Ava Pearson said:

> Mother's help was West Indian. She has often said we just couldn't have survived without her. . . . I had been raised in a home where my mother had always had household help. And I think it was something I just anticipated. Also, I did not like to do household cleaning. I don't get any gratification from it and I don't do it very well. I must have been very careful not to learn to do it.

Susan Keplin agreed:

> In those days, I was raised very spoiled. I never did a thing because we always had live-in help at home. And when I married, I don't know. My husband's family had had live-in help too. And we were just accustomed to it.

> It's not that I really disliked housework; I was just used to the freedom.

Note that the early expectation of having help with housework can lead to a real (though deliberately cultivated) dependency.

Even those who did not articulate this expectation must have been influenced by seeing their mothers run a house with the help of outsiders. And this fact underlies the importance of modelling, the learning of behaviors (and attitudes and emotional responses) by identifying with models. It may appear too obvious even to state that behavior must be conceptualized before it can be executed, but the consistency between the behavior of my interviewees and that of their mothers emphasizes the importance of such "observational learning" and, on the group level, of tradition.[4]

But this is not to deny that some women might have been motivated away from employing domestic help because of what they observed as children. John Green's comments illustrate the potential repulsing effect of modelling:

> I would never hire anyone to take care of my kids. I wouldn't want them to feel the same sense of anger and frustration I felt because I or my wife wasn't around. And I don't think I'd want someone to clean for me. For political reasons: I think it's sadistic. I would never objectify anyone like that. It's a master-slave relationship in its purest form, in a sense.

The women I interviewed were, by definition, women who chose to hire household help. For that reason, it is beyond the scope of this study to examine the attitudes of women who have chosen not to assume their mothers' role. It should be pointed out, however, that such women undoubtedly exist. Perhaps, as Albert Bandura's research on modelling suggests, the degree to which the behavior is imitated depends on the perceived rewards or punishments associated with it.[5] In any case, the women I interviewed emulated their mothers' behavior, and this emulation supports the contention that identification with models and tradition were highly significant factors in influencing the role choices of the women in my study.

Were practical need and tradition the only reasons the women chose to employ household help? Not at all. When Daniel Sutherland explored the motivations of nineteenth-century American women for hiring servants, he identified four:

> The physical strain of housework was the principal one. Many women simply could not accomplish their innumerable household tasks without help. Almost as important were the roles and responsibilities assigned to American women, especially their roles as "housekeepers" and "ladies." Status was the third reason for having servants, tradition yet another.[6]

While the weight of these might have shifted since the last century (for example, the "physical strain of housework" has been eased by household technology and commercial services), all of these motives appear still to hold true for women today. In addition to feeling the need for assistance with housework and conforming to tradition, modern women, too, hire domestics to free themselves for their "roles and responsibilities" as middle-class women and to confirm their status.

The social demands of today include not only the traditional volunteer work, community involvement, and cultural activities of the nineteenth-century matron but also jobs, both for economic necessity and for fulfillment. Margaret Slater, for example, first employed domestic help in 1955, when her first child was born. Though her maternal responsibilities are over, she still hires a once-a-week cleaner for the house in which only she and her husband now live. This allows Ms. Slater to put her energies into her job (teaching reading) and other more interesting and socially valued activities:

> I don't mind doing housework myself. But this house is very big and if I can get some help, it frees up some time for me to do other things. The problem isn't my disliking housework—although I can't say I get a big bang out of it either—but the problem is my limited time. I'm doing so many things, it seems.

While lower-income working women use daycare, family, and friends for childcare, and maintain their own houses during non-working hours, more affluent working women ease the burdens of this two-job lifestyle by hiring domestic help. And since "an increasing proportion of the wives entering the paid labor force comes from more affluent families,"[7] it may be assumed that a growing sector of the domestic-employing group is composed of working women. The director of a one-year-old employment agency in Newton, which places domestics exclusively, supports this view:

> The typical employer today is a professional woman married to a professional man, with children, working full time. Newton has many husband-wife doctor households, for example. I think the demand for domestics is increasing, not decreasing. I mean, look at our agency. And I know of two long-established employment agencies that have added domestic divisions during the one year we've been in business—because the demand is increasing.

Domestic May Lund agreed:

> Twenty years ago, most of the people you worked for were over forty and the women were at home. Today, they're young career women and a lot don't even have children. They just don't want to spend their time cleaning house; they want to give their time to their careers. . . . The feminist movement is causing white women to demand more household help.

As a result of the women's movement, the expectation of young middle-class women is that they will have careers whether there is family economic need or not. But this dramatic change in women's roles in the workplace has not been accompanied by a significant change in their attitudes toward their roles at home. The middle-class women I interviewed were not demanding that their husbands play a greater role in housekeeping; they accepted the fact that responsibility for domestic maintenance was theirs, and they solved the problem of their dual responsibilities by hiring other women to assist.

Confirmation of status, too, still motivates women to hire domestics. As might be expected, employers had little to say about that. Only Holly Woodward, in describing the regular complaining of her friends about their domestics, made what could be interpreted as a reference to domestics used for status: "I did not like the conversations where people sat around bitching about their help. . . . Some of it would be nouveau riche, just showing off. You know, how we suffer from the lower classes." Domestics, however, had no doubt about this motivation, and more than one said this was the reason some employers preferred black domestics to white. Odette Harris' comments are typical:

> She used to say I was more intelligent than her previous Irish girls. But I thought that the advantage of having a

> black girl is that it shows automatically that they have a maid. If somebody comes to the house and sees a black girl, they know she's a maid. Her mother would come to visit and she used to say, "I like a black girl." She told me! But I understand that what it is is we give them much more status.

Domestics as status symbols are certainly not new. Records from Rome indicate that some slaves performed no work but functioned solely to attest to their owners' status and wealth. Writing of the period between Augustus and Nero, when the extravagance in slaves (all of whom were domestic in Rome) reached its peak, R. H. Barrow states:

> The desire to rival a neighbour or friend led to the enlargement of slave staffs and the introduction of fresh extravagances and luxuries. . . . The mere multiplication of slaves becomes an ambition in itself; they must attend on walk or journey for mere appearance's sake. . . . The man of dignity must have his crowd of servants.[8]

In industrializing England and France, lackeys, coachmen, and footmen, often hired for their looks and dressed in ostentatious costumes, functioned solely to impress others. For the employer to be able to "waste" well-built male servants was seen as evidence of his extreme wealth. And for the not-so-wealthy upwardly mobile employers of the new English bourgeoisie developing in the mid-nineteenth century, having a "maid-of-all-work" served not only to impress others but also to convince the employers themselves of the legitimacy of their middle-class status. As Lenore Davidoff has observed: "The surest way of proving social superiority was to surround oneself with 'deference givers'; even specialized 'deference occupations.' . . . 'With one group, domestic servants, the middle class stood in a very special and intimate relationship: the one fact played an essential part in defining the identity of the other.'"[9]

Of the nineteenth-century American middle class, Sutherland wrote: "Americans were materialistic, . . . stricken by a feverish desire for material comfort and symbols of affluence that knew no cure save gratification. . . . It was nearly inevitable that Americans should accept servants as the ultimate means of 'conspicuous display.'"[10]

Since Americans remain a materialistic people, given to "conspicuous display" and judging themselves and others by externals as much now as in the nineteenth century, it may be assumed that the few employers and domestics who brought it up were indeed correct: the servant remains one of the desirable "symbols of affluence" with which upwardly striving Americans impress one another. In domestic May Lund's words: "It makes them feel good and look good if they have a black maid in the house. It makes them feel good at the office if they can say, 'Oh, ya, I left my girl working. I hope my girl remembers to do this, that and the other.'"

And as for Sutherland's fourth reason, though Americans have not been viewed as "tradition-directed" people, we have seen that tradition, maintained through the process of identification with models, remains an important factor in perpetuating the mistress-servant labor arrangement.

Thus, the reasons for hiring household help are many—and often interdependent. What Sutherland observed about nineteenth-century middle-class American women is indeed still true today:

> Families that had employed servants in one generation continued to enjoy their services in later generations. Women raised in such families became increasingly

> dependent on servants, and in time, family traditions became irrevocably enmeshed with ideas of status and fashionable living. Once accustomed to a lifestyle requiring servants, people found it hard to give them up. Even when the advent of modern household machines made housemaids obsolete on the practical level, status and tradition insured that some families would keep servants to operate the machines.[11]

If the subjects of my study are typical, practical need, the wish to be released for more valued activities, the desire for a status symbol, and tradition remain primary motivations for hiring domestic servants. But they are not the only reasons: our examination of the interpersonal dynamic between the employer and the employee will reveal additional motivations that have to do with psychological and ideological roles played by the kind of relationship that is typical between the women.

Becoming a Domestic

The twenty domestics I interviewed ranged in age from twenty-five to eighty-two. Their educational levels ranged from the third grade to three years of college. Eleven were doing domestic work at the time of the interviews: two had retired directly from it; the others were in other kinds of employment (like hospital housekeeper, matron in a women's shelter, daycare attendant, and director of a homemaking agency). Seventeen of the women had spent their youth in the rural or small-town South; one (of Cape Verdean heritage) grew up on Cape Cod; one grew up on an island in the West Indies; and the lone urbanite was born in Boston.

As we have seen in the previous chapter, domestic servitude has existed for millennia. But it has always been a low-prestige, low-reward position and remains so today. Why would twentieth-century women enter such an occupation? On a group level, the essential reasons are clear: economic need and limited alternatives. But on the individual level, other factors may have come into play and influenced the woman's decision to become a domestic worker.

We know that the employment opportunities of all women have been severely limited historically. The fact that domestic servitude was the single largest occupational category for all nineteenth-century American women is a reflection of the lack of educational and job opportunities for American women at that time. But, as the historical review revealed, the job marketplace began to expand for women around the turn of the century (an expansion accelerated by World War I) and those with more skills and more education and those who were white were able to move into factories, clerical work, and other kinds of employment. Black women, who had constituted 28.8 percent of the domestic servant sector during the nineteenth century, came to represent 45.8 percent by 1920.[12] (And in the early part of this century, as today, domestic service was an important occupation for Native American, Japanese-American, Mexican-American and other women of color.) For them, education was not a vehicle for escape; racist employment policies prevented their movement in any significant numbers into blue- and white-collar jobs until after World War II. It is small wonder, then, that the older women I interviewed explained the reasons for their entrance into domestic service so similarly; blatant racism in the job market apparently allowed no illusions of having a choice.

Eighty-two-year-old Anne Ryder, who came to Boston in the 1920's and immediately went into domestic service, said:

> I did it because I had to. There wasn't nothing else a colored woman could do then. They didn't pay nothing in

> those days: twenty-five cents an hour. Two dollars a day. Just imagine! And they tried to work us like slaves. If they had a thousand dollars they wouldn't pay you but twenty-five cents an hour. But there wasn't nothing else I could do.

Fifty-seven-year-old Boston-born Jane Louis, who entered live-in domestic service in Newton when she was seventeen, said:

> There were other things that I would have preferred to do. I would have liked to have been a teacher or a horticulturalist if I could. . . . I know a butler who has started his own butler service. But he's white. With us, we couldn't do those things. Practically every black woman in her fifties has done it. In Boston, if you weren't a domestic, you were an elevator person. And I'd rather do domestic work than run an elevator.

Marva Woods started working in South Carolina in the early 1930's. At age ten, she started cleaning houses part-time after school; she became a full-time domestic at age thirteen:

> My daddy died when I was six and my mother raised five children so I wanted to help her. At first I worked for three hours every day after school for three dollars a week. When I started full-time, I was making five dollars a week. I didn't have any choice!

And sixty-five-year-old Nell Kane reported that when she began domestic work in the 1930's in Florida

> we only got seven dollars a week. We worked from eight A.M. to five P.M. Monday through Saturdays. Of course, the cost of living wasn't what it is today. You could kind

> of survive. We thought, "Well, that's what the pay is, so. . . ." And there just wasn't any other kind of work.
>
> I would've liked to have continued my education. But when I was younger I didn't have the privilege of continuously staying in school. Because I lost my mother in my early years and was raised by a stepmother who was very selfish. I used to cry because I couldn't go to school. I remember the times I would have to stay home and help her with the ironing and washing. She would take in washing and ironing during those times. I remember many times when she had a lot of work to do, it was nothing for her to say "you stay home today." And I remember many times I shed many tears because I couldn't go to school.
>
> There were many others things I would have liked to do. Maybe to teach or maybe go ahead on and get a business course. But by lacking the proper education, that's why I went mostly to domestic work. There wasn't anything much you could do but housework in order to survive.

From those women who entered the labor market more recently, however, one hears more varied reasons and some sense of choice. Thirty-seven-year-old Edith Lincoln had done factory work and hospital housekeeping in Boston before switching back to the domestic service she had previously done at home on the Cape:

> Part-time housekeeping was easier with small kids. Ruth was four then and Vera was just a baby. And I like the freedom of it. I didn't like having to work from nine to five. I wanted to spend more time with the kids. . . . I like domestic work because it gives me time to do what I

> want. My family relations are better than my friends' and sisters'. These are the things I focus on. I don't have half the problems they have. No, I don't like nine-to-five jobs.

And thirty-seven-year-old May Lund went into day housecleaning soon after her arrival in Boston because of similar childcare concerns:

> I was at the belt factory but babysitting was becoming a problem. I couldn't find nobody to keep [her three-and-a-half-year-old son] the half a day he wasn't in kindergarten. So that's when I went into domestic work. That was a job where you could make your own hours.

Thirty-eight-year-old Florence Motley, whose light housekeeping job includes care of an elderly family member, stated:

> I like taking care of people. I used to work in a hospital as a nurse's aide. But I didn't like that. I quit because the care wasn't good; they wasn't half feeding the patients. I like this better. It's not hard and I like helping people, doing things for people.

Though some of the younger women talked about lack of job opportunities, they did so in geographic terms. For example, Edith Lincoln had become a live-in domestic at age sixteen because "on the Cape, black women were only chambermaids and domestics." And May Lund's decision to leave the South had to do with the "lack of job opportunities in a small town in Maryland." But these women were aware of wider opportunities in cities and, though they chose domestic service when they moved to Boston, being in a locale with more job alternatives appears to have been part of the attraction of Boston.

In addition to the reasons articulated by the women—the lack of alternatives, the convenience of the hours, and their preference for the work—there are two additional characteristics common to most of the women interviewed that I feel influenced their entering domestic service: their mothers' having been domestics, and their rural and small-town backgrounds.

As with employers, domestics learned by observing their mothers' behavior. All of the mothers of the domestics I interviewed, except one, had been domestics themselves.[13] For the younger and more educated women, in particular, who were conscious of having alternative employment open to them, one can appreciate the influence of childhood observations. Pat Owens was explicit about her mother's influence on her. As a teenager in the South, Ms. Owens had helped her mother serve at large parties. Years later, after her arm was burned at her job in a commercial laundry in Watertown, Ms. Owens decided to switch to domestic work

> because I used to like to see my mother work. I used to like to see her make different salads. I used to like to see her set a beautiful table . . . and the crystal . . . and the china. Well, she worked for a very wealthy family and I enjoyed doing what I did. So I says, "I'll go on and start doing domestic work."

But observation can repel; if behavior is perceived as eliciting more punishment than reward, it is less likely to be imitated. Undoubtedly, there are daughters of domestics who were motivated to stay away from such work because of what they observed their mothers experiencing.[14] But the predominance of women, both employers and domestics, who grew up with models for their present roles attests to the importance of observational learning in the role choices of young people and, thus, in the maintenance of tradition.

The domestics' being of rural and small-town backgrounds may have influenced their choice in two ways.[15] Domestic service historically has been more acceptable to rural people; poor urbanites hold the occupation in lower esteem. There was no indication from my interviewees that their families disapproved of their going into domestic work. Yet, now urban themselves, none of them would want their daughters to become domestics. For recent migrants to an urban area, this type of job does offer a place to live as well as work. It is for them neither a loss of status nor a compromise of family values. The transition from Southern farm to Southern or Northern city, from rural New England to Boston, or from a West Indian island to the urban Northeast was indeed cushioned by having basic practical needs, to some degree, met.[16] That all of the women interviewed who went into domestic service before age twenty-five went into a live-in situation as soon as they left their parents' home cannot be overlooked.

Because this occupation has been ethnically and racially ghettoized in this country, it is true that in the past many urban-born and better-educated black women have done domestic work, but my suspicion is that it was psychologically easier for the rural and less-educated women. Their family, their peers, and their social milieu did not share the low valuation of the job of those closer to or in the mainstream of the society. And recall McBride's suggestion that live-in domestic work in nineteenth-century England and France called for "values of dependence that the city did not breed."[17]

Various factors relating to time, place, and individual situations have contributed to these women's entering and remaining in domestic work, but it is clear that one underlies all others. For those who entered the labor market before World War II and/or in the South, there were few alternatives. The responses of the older women I talked with reflected that reality: a strong sense of entrapment was expressed. Most attributed it to race; a few to lack of education. But none expressed any feeling of choice. This was less true of the younger women. Many of them had done other types of work (typically factory work and hospital housekeeping) and had chosen domestic work at a certain point because of perceived benefits. But some of these same women have since moved into other occupations.

Of the eleven women still in domestic work and two who "retired"[18] directly from it, none had a high school diploma; the range of educational attainment was from the third to the eleventh grade with the mode around the eighth grade.[19] Of those who had moved out of domestic work, four were high school graduates and the range was from the eleventh grade through three years of college. The work patterns of the women in my study were consistent with national trends: as the labor market expanded for black women, those who remained in domestic service were there either by a conscious choice (and, more often than not, temporarily) or because of limitations caused by their class, particularly educational, backgrounds.[20] Thus the salient reason for women remaining in domestic service any length of time was the same as for entering it: economic need and limited alternatives.

Being an Employer

As a group, employers had less to say than did domestics about housework as an activity and the occupation of domestic service. This was not unexpected: for the domestics, many hours of their days and evenings were spent doing some kind of housework; for the employers, fewer hours were given over to such activity, they always exercised control over the length and intensity of their own housework, and domestics were a peripheral part of their lives. None of the employers I interviewed did all of her own cleaning; by contrast, all of the domestics, including eighty-two-year-old Anne Ryder, did theirs. Most employers expressed positive or neutral attitudes toward housework itself but a few expressed extreme dislike. And there was an interesting correlation between employers' attitudes toward doing housework and their views of it as an occupation. For example, Cheryl Dowd, Frances Stewart, and Pamela Kane all said they enjoyed doing housework. And when I asked Ms. Dowd what she thought of domestic work as an occupation, she said: "I think it's a pleasant occupation. It pays good—anywhere from six to ten dollars. You're usually in pleasant surroundings. And you're your own boss; you're fairly independent. It gives you time to think; its mindless. It's also a good way to get exercise." Ms. Stewart held a similarly positive view: "Well, it's a lot better than clerical work. It's less boring, there's less supervision, you're in a much prettier environment, you have more leeway. You can even use the TV at will!" And Pamela Kane, one of the two employers paying the highest salary I encountered (ten dollars an hour)—explained her attitude toward the occupation this way:

> Domestic work is something I would do myself, under certain circumstances. It combines satisfaction and money. It's a good job if it fits into your life. Not for a career though; it's hard work and there's no security. . . . I don't think, at this point in my life, that I'd be willing to hire anybody to come into my home where I was paying them less than what I make. It feels like a woman's issue, in some way. I suppose it's a political stance.

On the other hand, Alberta Putnam's aversion to housework is quite strong:

> I don't enjoy it. When we first moved up here, I did it all myself. But I really don't enjoy doing housework. . . . All my life I've fought against doing "women's work.". . . Even when the baby was born and I was at home all the time, I wanted help even more because I had this fear of falling into a housewife routine.

And she expressed the lowest regard of domestic work of all the women I interviewed: "Domestic work is nothing. I guess I look down on it because the people are not using their brains. . . . I always felt I was paying too much because the work is so *dumb*!"

Employers varied in their sensitivity to the circumstances that historically have caused women to go in to domestic service. A few, like Alice Lynch, seemed oblivious to the limitations on opportunity caused by class and race:

> I think it's a good service. It's perfectly all right to get money that way. It's not a very uplifting career; that is, I don't think it furthers your mental development in any way. If someone was doing it for a lifetime, I would think they hadn't very much ambition.

A few, like Susan Keplin, June Gordon and Ava Pearson, were exceptionally sympathetic:

> I think domestic work is lousy! I think the people who do domestic work only do it because they don't have the education to do anything else. They need money and this is one thing they can do. I wouldn't want to do somebody else's laundry, somebody else's dirty dishes. It's so menial. I'm sure if these women could have found any other kind of work to do, they would have done it. (Ms. Keplin)

> I have a hard time believing that anyone enjoys cleaning. People hold the occupation in low esteem because it's dirty work. And they have a low esteem for anybody that gets dirty when they work. I mean, garbagemen, you think of them as low because they get dirty and have to deal with unclean things. The same with domestic work. (Ms. Gordon)

> You have to wonder why people do this kind of work. It is certainly not the most gratifying. People went into this work not as a matter of choice, in many instances. It was sort of the bottom of the barrel. (Ms. Pearson)

And one, fifty-two-year-old Holly Woodward, showed considerable political awareness:

> I think the ethical questions involved the women's movement and the exploitation involved in one woman feeling that she should be free from the shit-work at home and requiring somebody else to do that. . . . I realize I have a problem hiring help because of my guilt and my concern about exploiting people, the colonial issue. I've read Fanon; it's all there. . . . Can you have a business-like deal in a house? . . . Who would put up with that shit by choice? Why would you choose something that's low-paid, that doesn't give you protection and that doesn't give you status? And there's so little pleasure in it!

Most of the employers, however, were at neither of these extremes.

In evaluating the typicality of the views of my interviewees, this may be an appropriate place to consider the self-selection that is applicable to research based on volunteer respondents. In addition to my subjects' being disproportionately Jewish and more educated than is the total population of white female employers, it may be assumed that those who would volunteer to be interviewed would be women whose perception of their behavior as employers was positive, who felt no shame about their treatment of their servants, and who would thus not be risking embarrassment or discomfort by answering probing questions about their experiences. Though this self-selection process yielded women with a wide range of attitudes and experiences, unquestionably women whose behavior as employers was extremely exploitive, abusive, or unpleasant would not volunteer to expose such behavior. Such women are unquestionably a minority; it may be assumed that most employers are not extreme in their attitudes toward and treatment of domestics. But while my small sample undoubtedly includes representatives of the minority who are exceptionally generous, egalitarian, and humane, it does not include women who are exceptional in the opposite way. For this reason, too, the employers I interviewed may be considered to represent the more liberal and progressive sector of the white female employing population.

When I asked employers what they looked for when hiring domestic help, personality characteristics were mentioned more often than job-related abilities. The responses of Cheryl Dowd and Sylvia Peabody were typical:

> I look for honesty and conscientiousness. . . . I wouldn't feel comfortable with someone coming in on a regular basis unless they were warm. I think of help as a friend helping more than I do a more formal relationship. (Ms. Dowd)

> I look for someone trustworthy and friendly, someone I'm comfortable with. (Ms. Peabody)

But there were variations related to the employer's place in life and needs. When Holly Woodward and Mary Beck wanted childcare they emphasized warm personalities.

> What I was always looking for was a style of childcare and a relationship to me rather than great skills, particularly in a young person. I can train them to do the work but I can't train them to be pleasant. (Ms. Woodward)

> They didn't last long if they came and it was obviously just a job. If I was leaving kids with them, they had to show warmth and affection. (Ms. Beck)

Those not needing childcare but with careers, like Jocelyn Minor and Elsa Coleman, emphasized reliability, honesty, and efficiency.

> I think that honesty is the most important thing . . . because . . . you're letting a person into your home. Reliability, it turned out, was *the* most important quality of the woman who is now working for me. It's her reliability that's made my job possible. If I had to call up and say, "I can't make it today," would I have gotten tenure? I doubt it. (Ms. Minor)

> My highest priority when I'm hiring help is reliability. And someone I can feel comfortable having in my house. (Ms. Coleman)

And women without careers or companionship needed the most from their domestics. Sixty-two-year-old Susan Keplin, who has never worked and is now widowed, talks revealingly about her domestic:

> She's a very nice lady, . . . [a North Carolina-born black woman from Dorchester] and she's been with me for

about ten years. She's probably in her fifties; you can't really tell. She's very loyal and very wonderful and I love her. . . . She gets one paid vacation day each year. We eat lunch together on the day she works; she's my friend. It hasn't always been like that; it's this particular woman. She's taken care of me. She's one of the family. . . .

She's very honest. She's very clean. She's *very* loyal. She's intelligent though she hasn't had much schooling. . . .

She doesn't clean very well, you know, but I would never think of letting her go. I don't know, I really like her. She never comes to work on time but that's all right. We have a great relationship. She knows me so well. . . . I always give her clothes. I'm sure she takes food. At times I've given her furniture. When she knows I'm cleaning out things, she asks for what she wants. She's not bashful. But she's not going to get everything she wants. . . .

She has her own room here. She knows she can stay here anytime. Sometimes when she works late for one of her other employers or when the weather is bad and she doesn't want to make the trip to Dorchester, she'll call and say, "I'm coming." It's fine with me. She'll always have a room here.

If I were hiring her brand new, didn't know her, I wouldn't keep her. Coming late, not cleaning very well. But if she left, I'd have a hard time finding someone else. It's worth much more to me to have her loyalty and her trust. And know if I'm sick, she'll come and take care of me, know I can count on her being there. That's much more important than the cleaning.

Ms. Keplin's emphasis on personality reflects her needs: her lack of companionship with some physical problems creates the need for her domestic to function as friend and nursemaid more than cleaner.

John Green, the young man who grew up with a series of maids, watched his mother behave similarly and, even at fourteen, understood why:

> We moved to South Carolina when I was about thirteen or so. And the second year we were there, we got a woman named Ella. She and my mother were very, very close. My mother felt very warmly toward her. . . . Though I thought my mother was kind of condescending toward her, patronizing really. My mother was extremely lonely then. And that had a lot to do with it. She was looking for some kind of companionship because all of her friends were back in New York. I think that was a big part of why they got so close.

And recall Margaret Slater, who, as a young mother whose husband was away frequently, hired Ann "partly to help me take care of the baby and partly because I didn't like being alone so much." Such relationships suggest another motive for hiring domestic help: to meet emotional needs of the employer (in these cases, the need for companionship), needs that can change over time. What Ava Pearson describes for herself appears to be a common process:

> Right now [that the children are grown], I don't want closeness. I think there's a difference when you have young children. Then you want to know the person and her ideas and you want her to know you, to really help you. With my job and my activities now, I don't need a friend, I need the work done.

The needs of young mothers and of retired women, particularly if widowed, cause exceptional emphasis on personality traits of the domestic worker.

Employers' statements on what they look for in domestics make it clear that, in most cases, it is far more than an adequate job performance; they want a particular kind of personality and relationship. Domestics have more to say, as we shall see, about what personality traits and behaviors employers want. At this point, what is important to note is employers' emphasis on the personality as well as the job skills of the domestic.

The relationship between the women ranged not only from intense to distant but not surprisingly from enjoyable to quite unpleasant, the latter usually of short duration. The older employers, in particular, who had had extensive experience with a number of domestics, usually had one or two problem situations to relate. The two types most frequently cited were drinking and stealing. The stories of Jocelyn Minor, Karen Edwards, and Alice Lynch describe situations of domestics' drinking:

> There was one really unpleasant episode. The liquor cabinet was upstairs. I was downstairs visiting with a friend. And she was upstairs, I thought taking care of the house. And when I came up, she was drunk. And so my friend stayed at home with the children and I tried to get this woman home. I tried to take her home but I didn't know where she lived. I didn't know what to do. I finally took her to the police station. I said I have to get home; I have to take care of the kids. The reason this incident comes back to haunt me is because three years ago I came to the realization that I had become an alcoholic. And I keep thinking of that poor woman and what's become of her. (Ms. Minor)

> Another Irish woman was drinking my husband's scotch while she was on the job and replacing it with water. She never seemed drunk. It took us a while to figure out what was happening. When I finally accused her, she denied it. But I knew that's what was happening so I let her go. (Ms. Edwards)

> She came two days a week, did the cleaning and ironing. . . . She would also come and help at parties. We had a lot of parties. People had cocktail parties in those days, served a lot of martinis. So she would get rather high during the evening. But those were special occasions. It didn't matter too much. . . . We had another one in Chicago who drank from our liquor cabinet. It was her behavior that gave her away more than the missing liquor; she seemed definitely tipsy by the end of the day. I let her go. (Ms. Lynch)

And the stories of Frances Stewart, Carolyn Oxford, and Karen Edwards describe situations of domestics' stealing:

> Theresa was taking coins from my pocketbook. It took me a long time to notice that there was a small amount of money regularly missing. But once I figured it out, I just fired her. It just made me very nervous about what else she took, what she did and what she didn't do. (Ms. Stewart)

> Probably the most unpleasant experience I had was when I discovered this woman was taking pieces of my clothing and storing them at her mother's house. I didn't realize what was going on for a long time. If I couldn't find an article I'd think it must be dirty or at the cleaners.

> Finally, when I was missing a very good jacket I became concerned. I looked in her room and found some of my things. . . . When she came home, I confronted her. I told her that I was angry about it. At first, she denied it. So we went to her room and I had her open her drawers. I told her that I had already looked in her room and I explained to her why. . . . The whole thing was very unpleasant. I was very accusatory. We went to her mother's. Her mother at first denied everything. It was so unpleasant. (Ms. Oxford)

> I had two high school girls from Wellesley taking care of the children two nights a week and cleaning on Saturdays. They worked for about a year and a half. They were regularly stealing gold, cash, and clothes—even one of my fancy nightgowns. I didn't realize it for a long time. My husband and I would have an argument every Monday about a few dollars being missing, but we didn't suspect them. Then another high school girl revealed what had been going on. I called the girls' parents and the police. But one of the girls had an uncle on the force so everything was hushed up. I didn't press charges; in Wellesley, you don't do that. . . . Other people who have cleaned for me have stolen things too: money and jewelry. Whenever I discovered it, I dismissed the people immediately. (Ms. Edwards)

A few other kinds of problems, less frequently mentioned, are noteworthy because of what they reveal about employers' judgments of domestics: poor hygiene . . .

> She had just come from Puerto Rico. She was like a wild kid. Didn't have the slightest notion of American

hygiene in the kitchen. At night, she would urinate in the waste basket. And there was a toilet right near her room. . . . I always had a picture of her around a campfire. . . . These girls were very unfinished products, you know. Eighteen, nineteen, twenty. (Holly Woodward)

. . . low morals . . .

I had a series of different people, live-in. . . . They weren't the best people; they weren't the best types. Perhaps because at that time I couldn't afford real high-type help. . . . I had one that used to bring men into her room. We came home one night and there was a man in her room. And my husband didn't like that. So we had to fire her. (Susan Keplin)

. . . and poor attitudes, attitudes that might reflect only an unwillingness to take orders unquestioningly . . .

I told her to take off the tablecloth and put it away. She said why take it off when it's going right back on. She finally did it but I said, "There's no point in this. If you don't agree with somebody, keep it to yourself; you're working for me. . . ." Since she wouldn't do what I asked her to do, since I'm paying someone to do this. . . . So I let her go that day. (Susan Keplin)

. . . or an intense political anger:

He came only a couple of months. He was foreign-born. Maybe from Denmark. One day a week. I seem to remember I was paying him sixteen dollars for four hours. . . . He was sort of a hostile angry fellow who had made me feel pretty uncomfortable. He used to make a lot of nasty comments that made me feel uncomfortable, like about the size of the house and that we were only three people living in it and, you know, what a waste. He just made me feel very uncomfortable. . . . So when he called to say he wanted more hours and more money and we told him that was surpassing our budget, I wasn't terribly disappointed at that parting of the ways. (Elsa Coleman)

That was a very tense relationship. Carol worked for us during Attica. And it was a good thing the kids were more independent by then because her anger was vast. And there were times when I felt like a therapist but I didn't therapize. I remember incidents. Once she put something through the washing machine that left it coated with fuzz. And I said, "Gee, you'd better not put another load in until you clean it out." And she turned to me and she said, "How do you expect me to clean it out? Scrub it with my hands?" I didn't know what she was so angry about. But it became apparent during Attica. She couldn't hold herself in. She poured out what white people do to black people. . . . And that gave me some perspective. I didn't take it personally. She was really furious and who am I to say she shouldn't be. But that doesn't mean it was easy for me to be on the receiving end of her cracks. (Holly Woodward)

But it should be borne in mind that stories of such problems were not the norm. By far, most of the relationships the employers discussed would be described as comfortable and satisfactory, neither problematic nor extraordinarily positive.

Employers' preferences are interesting in what they reveal about employers' concerns. There was variation in ethnic and racial preferences (even individuals could vary in their preferences, depending on what household task was to be done), but all agreed on their preference for an individual worker over a cleaning service, and no employer preferred a man over a woman. What is interesting about these choices—expressed either directly or by employing patterns—is that they all, in some way, relate to the kind of relationship the employer wishes to establish.

Ethnic and racial preferences were, not unexpectedly, hardest to get at. Only three employers admitted to a bias on the basis of race or ethnicity. One was thirty-two-year-old June Gordon:

> I wouldn't hire a hispanic. I've seen their neighborhood in Waltham. They're dirty. Their cars are dirty. And the people and children are not well taken care of. I would avoid hiring a hispanic. That would be the only ethnic group I would avoid.

Another was seventy-two-year-old Jennifer Evans:

> I don't want any more colored help. They don't do everything they're supposed to do. They're lazy, you know. I used to work with a lot of them at the hospital and they think nothing of not showing up if their children are sick or something. . . . Do you know any place where I could get some help that wasn't colored?

And the third was forty-four-year-old Karen Edwards:

> I advertised in suburban newspapers for childcare and cleaning. I didn't use the *Globe* because I wanted middle-class help who would take very good care of my children. I wanted the babysitter to be another mother, a woman like me, which means middle-class, suburban, and white.

However, we can speculate about the issue further, based on the clue that Karen Edwards offers above: might employers' using suburban newspapers and avoiding the *Boston Globe* be, in some cases, an indication of a wish to avoid domestics of color? Certainly, a number of my interviewees, like Cheryl Dowd, Pamela Kane, and Carolyn Oxford, volunteered that they located help only through suburban newspapers. Why?

> I only looked in the *Arlington Advocate* because I would want to hire someone locally. (Ms. Dowd has had no Third World domestics.)

> She answered an ad I had put in the *Wellesley Townsman.* I only advertise in that paper because I didn't want to have to pick somebody up. (Ms. Kane has had no black help.)

> I usually check the ads in the Wayland and Framingham papers. . . . I don't check the *Globe* because I'd have to get into picking the person up. And the classified section's too big. (Ms. Oxford has had domestic help for twenty years and has never hired a black person.)

But the issue of ethnic and racial preference is not a simple one in domestic service. There are strong indications that many employers prefer whites for childcare, in particular. Karen Edwards was the only interviewee to say this explicitly—"I wanted the babysitter to be . . . a woman like me, . . . middle-class, suburban, and white"—but her comment is particularly noteworthy because she was the only interviewee who did not know my race (the interview was conducted on the telephone). Even stronger evidence of this preference comes from national figures for the job category breakdown within domestic service. While over 60 percent of white domestics were childcare workers in 1979, only 10.5 percent of black domestics were. By contrast, 73 percent of blacks were "cleaners and servants," while 30.3 percent of whites were.[21] These figures undoubtedly reflect in part the choices of domestics themselves; a higher proportion of whites are under twenty-five, single, and working part-time. But my research suggests that the figures also reflect attitudinal preferences of employers. Perhaps part of what employers like Jocelyn Minor meant when they said things like "I do look for more in childcare people than in cleaning people" was that they see whites as "more" (refined, articulate, potentially upwardly mobile, intelligent . . .) and prefer to have such people around their children.

And there is this additional dimension to ethnic choices that must be taken into account: some employers actually prefer women of color as servants because (according to my domestic interviewees) their presence makes the employers' status clearer to neighbors and because (according to my analysis developed fully in Chapter 5) women of color function better as contrast figures for strengthening employers' egos and class and racial identities.

Thus, the motives behind racial and ethnic choices in domestic service are complex and varied. Employers may avoid or choose women of color because of unhealthy attitudes about race. What is certain is that employers of domestics, as overly conscious of race as all Americans, do not approach the establishment of this arrangement "color blind."

Employing patterns, as well as a few comments, clearly indicate that many employers prefer foreign-born help. The economic motive has already been discussed: historically and currently, foreign-born workers will accept lower pay than will Americans. But Holly Woodward's comments illustrate another reason foreign-born help is desirable:

> When we bought the house, one consideration was to be in an area where I could get Irish kids to come and live

> with me. . . . For me, they were easier to deal with than the black kids. The black women I could deal with. But there was nobody else, anyhow. It was either the Portuguese kids or. . . . The Irish weren't angry to be in this position because they had come from hell.

Foreign-born women, more vulnerable and less "angry" (or, at least, less apt to show it), are attractive to employers also because of their docility and more subservient manner. Many, from societies with more rigid class structures that lack the egalitarian philosophical underpinnings of the States, are more willing to display deferential behavior toward employers. And, as we shall see in the subsequent chapter, such behavior is appreciated and encouraged by employers. Employers' preference for foreign-born help not only emanates from their desire to pay as little as possible but is another indication of their wish to have a certain kind of relationship with the domestic, a relationship as important as the quality of the housework performance.

And employers' preference for an individual over a cleaning service further underscores this desire. None of my interviewees preferred a service because "they will not do everything," "these services are too expensive," or "I hate the impersonality." Indeed. The preference for an individual is in part a preference for an ongoing relationship. (Cleaning services send teams of workers that might change with each visit.)

And this finding suggests that the kind of relationship the employer prefers can only be established with another woman: no employer preferred a male worker over a female. The comments of Alice Lynch, Karen Edwards, and Ava Pearson were typical:

> I prefer women. Men don't do certain things. (Ms. Lynch)

> I've turned down males. I'm concerned with having a sexual deviant around my daughters. (Ms. Edwards)

> I think there's a sex difference. There are certain things that women have done for me that I wouldn't ask a man to do. Clean the refrigerator, for example. Men can do heavier things well. . . . There are certain things that a woman's nimble fingers might do. A man might be more clumsy. (Ms. Pearson)

Undoubtedly, women do work differently than men; undoubtedly, an individual worker will undertake tasks a cleaning service will not. But I submit that employers' preference for an individual woman over a man or a service also relates to their desire for a certain kind of relationship with the worker, a relationship that can only exist between women. Hearing domestics describe the relationships with employers yielded invaluable insights into the subtleties of that uniquely female interpersonal dynamic.

Being a Domestic

Domestic work is obviously a form of physical labor. The work yields some of the same satisfactions (for example, a sense of accomplishment) as well as many of the same problems (for example, exhaustion and physical disabilities). But domestic work is far more: as we have seen, to maneuver oneself into a satisfactory position—one not overly physically demanding, with more than minimal material benefits and with job security—one must have a pleasing personality as well as, if not more than, good housework skills.

Being a domestic means knowing the work and knowing the employers. It was not surprising that domestics had much more to say about housework, their employers, and the nuances of their relationships with them than employers did about housework and their relationships with domestics—so much of domestics' lives was spent intensely involved in these activities and relationships. Nor was it surprising that domestics considered the treatment they received from employers the most important aspect of the work. Research on women's values and morality indicates that women place more emphasis on the quality of their interpersonal relationships than on achievement. From the people in this historically degraded occupation, one which is further degraded when women or despised ethnic groups do it, it is not unexpected that we hear cries for dignity and humane treatment. Listen, for example, to Esther Jones . . .

> She didn't think I was human, the way she worked me.

. . . and to Edith Lincoln . . .

> How you get along with your employer is everything. If she treats you bad, your job's impossible.

. . . and to Nancy Clay:

> I just wanted them to treat me like a human being. That's all I asked.

Clearly, for most domestics, as for most employers, the relationship established with the other played a critical role in their satisfaction with the work situation. (The few exceptions were women—both domestics and employers—who seemed to prefer and create more distant, businesslike relationships, not usually possible or desired in a live-in, childcare, or full-time situation, rare even in part-time "day work.") How do domestics see their employers? What kind of relationship do they desire? What are their lives as domestics like?

It goes without saying that the relationship between mistress and servant is highly complex. Where strong dislike on either part developed, the relationship was sure to be short-lived. (Anne Ryder expressed the attitude I heard from both employers and domestics: "If they didn't treat me right, they didn't treat me long.") Transiency, as we have seen, has been a characteristic of domestic service since the late nineteenth century.

But those relationships that lasted often combined contradictory feelings, both fondness and dislike, respect and disdain, support and indifference. It is from those relationships, where the women had the opportunity to get to know one another well, that the richest material emerges. I have chosen five domestics' stories to provide the foundation for our understanding domestics' lives and views. These five were chosen because of their diversity of attitudes and experiences. As diverse as they are, however, patterns emerge—patterns of migration and transiency, of hard work and minimal compensation, of women being used by other women.

But before examining these lives, two findings from the interviews with domestics should be noted. First, none of the domestics disliked housework *per se* (as did some of the employers); no domestic minded doing her own housework, and most considered it an acceptable occupation. However, when I asked each woman near the end of the interview what her reaction would be if her daughter said she wanted to go into domestic work, all were adamantly opposed to the idea (including those few who found it a "pleasant" occupation).

Pat Owens and Marva Woods were two of the four domestics who were very positive about their occupation. Both women had mainly good things to say about domestic work; both women had the kind of personality—polite, slightly ingratiating, and lacking any hint of arrogance or anger—that must have been an asset to them in this occupation. I interviewed sixty-four-year-old Pat Owens in the kitchen of her top-floor apartment in a triple-decker in

Dorchester. Gracious and energetic, she fixed us tea, puttered in the kitchen, and spoke animatedly throughout the interview. The oven door stood open to provide us with heat (it was a below-freezing January day) and a pot boiled on top of the stove for humidity. Ms. Owens looked forward to retiring in a year and moving with her merchant marine husband to Florida. But now she works full-time as a domestic for members of two families, one of which she has been with (she uses the preposition "in") for almost thirty years. She talked about her work:

> I don't find nothing bad about domestic work. But I'll tell you one thing. It's only a certain type of person that I'll work for. [Ms. Owens here described applying for a day-work position where the woman asked her to enter through the back door because she liked her "maids" to do so. Ms. Owens told her she would not be anyone's personal maid and all of her other employers had thought enough of her to give her the keys to their front doors. She turned down this job offer.] I've been in one family for almost thirty years. First I worked for the mother and I'm still with the daughter. For a while I cleaned up the husband's costume jewelry place on Saturdays. The daughter I'm still working for lives in Chestnut Hill. One day Mrs. Smith said, "My daughter will be coming out of the hospital with her new baby. Will you give her a couple of weeks instead of coming to me?" I said "sure" and I'm still with her.
>
> I eat supper with the people I work for. We're like one big happy family. It's just like home. I'll be with them until I retire.

Ms. Owens went on to describe how one employer does her shopping for her at a discount food store (because "in these

Roxbury stores, the food isn't good and they charge you more")[22] and another gets meats for her once a month from a discount meat supply store. She told me about getting two birthday presents early: slacks and a (very inexpensive) toaster she pointed out to me. And as we sat in her oven-heated, clean, but dilapidated apartment in a poorly maintained triple-decker on a run-down street in Dorchester, she asked almost passionately, "How can you go wrong with people like that? How can you not *like* people like that?" (And remember that Ms. Owens' merchant marine husband helps support the apartment.)

Marva Woods says she has liked all of her jobs: cottonpicker, hotel cook, and for the longest time—twenty years—domestic servant. ("I just love to wash, iron and cook.") But there is an inconsistency between her positive words about her work and the aura of despair that surrounds her. Her only criticism of domestic work is the lack of medical coverage for illness. Otherwise, her jobs in both the South and the North were "real nice." A reticent, soft-spoken, and sad woman, with a Sphinx smile, deep dimples, and a youthful face that belies her sixty years, Ms. Woods's presence suggests a life of little joy and less opportunity for contacting and expressing her essence. She went to work part-time at age ten and full-time at thirteen to help her widowed mother, had to remain a live-in servant through an unsuccessful marriage and the births of two children ("I saw my husband on weekends and some afternoons"), and has raised her two children alone on consistently meager salaries. Recruited in South Carolina by a Chestnut Hill couple in the mid-1960's, she left her children with her mother to work for thirty-seven dollars a week—keeping ten dollars for herself and sending twenty-seven dollars home. Ms. Woods felt fortunate: she had never been given two weeks' paid vacation before or been supplied with a uniform and shoes. Though she regularly put in twelve- to fifteen-hour days and occasionally had to endure the mistress screaming at her (to which Ms. Woods could calmly respond, "Now don't holler at me, please"), she remained on this job for twelve years, leaving in 1977 with a pay of fifty-five dollars a week. Ms Woods's descriptions of two of her jobs typify her experiences and attitude:

> When we moved to a small town in South Carolina, I was sixteen. So I got a live-in job then. And I had to cook, wash, iron, and clean. I was making ten dollars a week [in 1938]. I worked days and evenings. They worked at the mill on the second shift. Sometimes they would work eleven 'till seven the next morning. So I would have to get the children ready for school and all. They treated me real nice. The husband would go hunting and kill rabbits and bring one for me. I'd take it to my mother's. They gave me clothes too. And a nice gift when I got married. I still lived in. I saw my husband on weekends and some afternoons. I'd go home on Saturday morning and didn't have to go back until Monday morning. I'd see him then. That job was fine. I worked for them about nine years. . . .
>
> The lady called me from Boston [in the mid-1960's]. She told me she was sending me a ticket. I came because it was better pay here. I was in Chestnut Hill. They was real nice to me. They had two children and a dog. She told me that on the phone; she said, "I hope you like dogs." They was real nice. . . . I was living in, like before, and I worked until I got the children to bed. . . . I had every Thursday and every other Sunday off. They furnished my uniform and my shoes and everything! She said she always furnished a uniform for her help.

> The children really liked me. And I liked them too. They was nice children and they behaved good. I was attached to them. . . .
>
> I worked there for twelve years. One of her friends came and said to me, "You're the only person who has stayed this long." They said she was hard to work for but I didn't have no problem. It was nice. . . . All my jobs was real nice.

Considering the poor conditions in which both of these women live—after a lifetime of hard work (forty years for Ms. Owens; fifty for Ms. Woods)—one cannot help but wonder how they remain so positive about their lives and work. But the positiveness of the two women is neither identical nor unexplainable. Pat Owens' appears more genuine; she seems to believe in the value of her work and the goodness of her employers' treatment of her. Ms. Owens has apparently convinced herself that her lot is fine. And the reality of her material poverty has been successfully blocked out in favor of her more positive version of her existence (a feat not to be underestimated for one who goes into affluent areas and homes daily). Marva Woods, on the other hand, was not as convincing. She seemed to be saying words she wanted both of us to believe so that she might avoid her own suspicions that her work and her life were less than successful, so that I might find in her experiences behavior worthy of respect. But I sensed a disharmony between her words and the feelings behind them, a disharmony that undoubtedly contributes to her essential sadness and lethargy.

But both women's ways of coping with desperately hard lives are understandable. Both in their sixties, having long ago released hopes of doing "something that would be upgrading," they are struggling to infuse by their attitudes a dignity into "careers" that they know the world around them finds valueless, unworthy of prestige, undeserving of reasonable pay. Noticeably lacking in these women was an expression of anger; strongly present was the desire to be liked. To convince themselves that their employers have treated them with respect and have paid them a fair wage and to be able consistently to elicit warm responses from others they encounter (including me) is to affirm to themselves that they merit respect, that their work has deserved fair compensation, and that they themselves are valuable because they are lovable. To create a career that was "real nice" is to create a self of worth. Socially safe because of the ingratiating personna it requires but psychologically fragile because of the discrepancies between reality and the women's versions of it, this is one possible way of coping with a life lived on the lowest strata of this society's class, race, and gender hierarchies.

More typical were the domestics who recognized both positive and negative aspects to domestic work. Esther Jones typifies these women. Ms. Jones likes housework quite a bit. (Her own apartment is immaculate and quite tastefully decorated, her appearance, demeanor, and dress unexpectedly elegant for an eighth-grade dropout from rural Alabama). Except for short-term jobs as a restaurant cook, factory worker, and hospital cleaner, she has done domestic work for most of her life: "I really like housework. I like keeping house. I like cooking. I think even if I had the education to do other work, there's only one other job I might like to do and that is be a nurse."

Ms. Jones describes her early jobs in Alabama positively but with some reservations:

> I did the cooking and washing, ironing and cleaning house. They had a little servants' house; I lived there. They treated me pretty good, I would say. I liked it . . . but you know, I was young; it was a job.

> Then I worked for a family, he raised horses. He had seven boys and one girl. I liked the job because the kids were very, very nice. I didn't feel like I was working. I felt like I was in the family then. 'Course I had to work. But they was just plain ordinary people.

Though she was making only four dollars a week at this live-out job in the mid-1940's, she felt

> it was enough money to live off at that time. And you know, that was what they were paying. And they gave you so much more! I mean, they gave you food. I don't mean just scraps, but good food. And you could get what you wanted. They didn't mind if you took it home, so mostly I didn't have any food to buy. At holidays, they would give me money. And they would give me used clothes because they was *good.* And, at that time, I was happy to get them; they seemed new to me! [Laughter] Yes, they really treated me well.

But of the five servant positions Ms. Jones has held since coming north, she considers only one a good experience. When I asked Ms. Jones why she said she "loved" this position, she responded: "Because she treated me just like another person, not like someone working for her. And the boy living at home, he was fifteen, and he was crazy about me and I was crazy about him. And the husband was even nice to me too." Note that her fondness for this job was based on the quality of the interpersonal relationships with family members; there was no mention of wages, duties, or other work-related issues. Ms. Jones left this position only because she wanted to move from New York to Boston, and when she left she and her employer "cried at the kitchen table."

Ms. Jones expressed her dissatisfaction with three subsequent jobs in Boston by leaving them; she has now reached an uneasy truce at a fourth. In 1962, she lived in Brookline with an older couple but quit because of overwork:

> I was cooking and cleaning. I would make him his breakfast before he went to business, then bring her breakfast to her in bed. In the evening, I would cook and serve dinner. I didn't eat with them; I'd eat my dinner afterwards in the kitchen.
>
> I quit right after Passover. There was all this work to do; everything had to be changed. She had hired a lady to come in and help her but at the last minute the lady called up and said she couldn't come. And she didn't try to get anybody else! I had to do all this work! I told her before we finished that when I finished putting the dishes away, that was it. It was too much work and she hadn't even tried to get anyone else. So I was finished.

Her next job in Wellesley ended after one year because her employer

> was tight with her money. I just didn't think she was paying me enough money.

Did you ask for a raise?

> No, I just left.

Though Ms. Jones had light housekeeping duties and no cooking on her next job in Newton,

> I didn't want to stay because it was too close. They didn't have no sleeping quarters. They didn't care. I was sleeping in a room right next to [that of] the sixteen-

year-old boy and I didn't like that. I hadn't been used to living that close. We had to use the same bathroom. The room was small. I stayed about six months. And that's the reason I left there: it was just too close.

For eighteen years now, Ms. Jones has worked for a Chestnut Hill family. Though her relationship with the wife has been unpleasant and Ms. Jones is passionate in her dislike of her (describing her as "mean," "a bitch," and "nasty"), she is intensely fond of the husband and children and says she has remained there because of her "friendships" with them. Through the years, she has maneuvered her way around the overly demanding personality of the wife and gained concessions (for example, getting the heavy cleaning done by a once-a-week cleaner) that have made the job worth keeping. Her friendships with the husband and children have yielded material as well as psychological benefits that encourage and support her. During illnesses, she has received expensive gifts (a color TV, a carpet) and expressions of caring ("He said, 'I am your friend and I worry about you.' See, *he* likes me. *He* appreciates what I do"). Though Ms. Jones's close relationship with the husband is untypical in this occupation, the fact that her strongest feelings about the job relate to people, and not to the work itself, is not.

Eighty-two-year-old Anne Ryder was the oldest woman I interviewed—and the most bitter about the occupation. She was one of the few women who questioned the acceptability of domestic work as an occupation: "Anybody who can get out of it, tell them don't do it. I mean, why should I go clean up your house when you can do it yourself? And why shouldn't you do it yourself?" And, despite her apparent high opinion of herself, she had little good to say about her life's work:

> I didn't do everything those folks told me to do. Some I did and some I didn't. They would tell me to get on my knees and scrub the floor and I didn't do it. I didn't mess up my knees. I told one lady, "My knees aren't for scrubbing. My knees are made to bend and walk on." I didn't have a lot of bumps and no black knees from scrubbing floors. I took care of myself.
>
> I had a girlfriend, she used to always leave work with her hands smelling like household ammonia. Now, I never put my hand in . . . I thought too much of my hands to put them in that stinking stuff. I didn't see where it made sense! Her hands all tough, hard, looking bad. She *worked.* Some of these girls really worked. But I slumped. I did what they told me to do; I did my job. If they didn't like it, they could let me go. I always felt I could get something to do.
>
> If I didn't like the job, I'd quit; if they didn't like me, they'd fire me.

It was not surprising that Ms. Ryder was never successful in acquiring one of the more privileged domestic positions. She has no hint of servility or obsequiousness about her; on the contrary, she has a self-possessed quality that could be, one would imagine, threatening to some employers. Ms. Ryder enjoyed telling me stories of her resistance to exploitation. Her self-respect was sometimes expressed in overt feistiness:

> I remember one Sunday morning, this woman told me to scrub her kitchen floor on my hands and knees. I got mad at her and said to her, "You sit right down there and wait until I scrub it." So I got a whole lot of ammonia and

> clorox and the stuff with the twin kids on the box. And I just poured it over the floor. And then half wiped it up. And you know what it looked like when I got finished! She just looked at that floor. That floor looked bad for two or three days. I wouldn't wash it 'cause I told her I'd already scrubbed it. That floor was so bad I didn't even like to walk on it 'cause it was muddy and sticky. If you ever washed with dirt cleanser, household ammonia, and clorox. . . . Finally, I did wash it. She had wanted me to get on my knees and scrub it. And I wasn't *thinking* about getting on my knees and scrubbing it. And, after that, I could just mop it up and it would look nice. No, my knees weren't made for walking all over the floor!

And sometimes in self-protective subterfuge:

> I did do the washing for her for a long time. But I got tired of it. So I didn't half rinse the soap out. And when you don't half rinse the soap out, the wash turns brown. I got it brown, then she told me she was going to get a woman in to do dayswork. So when this woman came in and started doing dayswork, the shirts and things looked so nice. But I could get it nice, you know; but I didn't want to overdo because I had enough work in the house to do without doing all that laundry. So I knew if I messed up on something, something had to go. So I messed up on the laundry. . . . I had to take care of myself.

But as determined as her efforts might be, Ms. Ryder could not avoid the exploitation that was an inherent part of this occupation: in her forty years of domestic work, she never got a paid vacation, was never paid when out sick, never had medical insurance, and left the field before it was covered by minimum wage legislation. It is extraordinary that, despite her low regard for the occupation ("What are you studying that for, anyway? There's nothing worth studying!") and her bitterness about her employers ("I didn't like any of them. I worked for them 'cause I had to"), she has been able to maintain her self-respect and avoid despair about her life.

Almost as angry as Anne Ryder, Elizabeth Roy was fortunate enough to have been born later and to have had the opportunity to move out of domestic work. After going through a training program run by a black women's service organization in Boston, Ms. Roy has become a matron in a women's shelter. And she also has become an activist for change in domestic service, speaking at seminars and attending conferences of the NCHE. But she remembers her first experiences as a domestic in Boston well:

> By me being from the South and not accustomed to the culture here, it made it extra difficult emotionally. There I was in Lexington. Out. Excluded from my people. You would see some when you came off for your two days off. They would try to fix it so you'd have Thursday and every other Sunday off. No two days together. After living in for a while, you really got the feeling of unusefulness to yourself. You just felt like you was bought over.

Ms. Roy had regular confrontations with her mistress, sometimes including mutual yelling, cursing, and threats. A final confrontation came about when Ms. Roy's fifteen-year-old son, whom she had brought up from the South, called her one morning from Roxbury to tell her he was too sick to go to school:

> Mrs. Grant hit the ceiling. She said, "I told you not to have anyone calling here asking for you in the morning! I'm going to have Dr. Grant speak to you." I said, "Well, you tell Dr. Grant, if my son can't call his mother, who in the hell *can* he call?" The books they read about the South was incorrect; I told her that. I said, "Since my son can't call here, I'm not obligated to you in no kind of way. My child comes first and I want you to know it. He comes even before you and your family—and I want you to know that." Well, she couldn't digest that! "So, now, here; here's your kitchen, you clean it, I'm going to see about my child." I upset her. See, she thinks Southern people are supposed to be dummies. It upset her so bad she didn't know that to do.

That evening the husband established an uneasy truce between the women. But that was shattered forever when Ms. Roy discovered a tape recorder had been placed in her bedroom:

> I discovered they had fixed up a tape recorder in my room that recorded my coming in and going out, conversations. Well, you talking about a black woman going off when I found out? What happened was, I had just come in the front door and I noticed him, he went straight upstairs as I came in. And, then one of the little boys [six years old] said, "Daddy has the tape recorder on."

Ms. Roy waited to talk to him but he left the house before she got a chance. The only adult at home was his sister and that evening, she confronted her:

> I said, "You tell him this. I worked for him two years and he didn't set up no tape recorder to tape my comings and

> goings and what I did here with his children. You tell him he has violated my civil rights and I know he doesn't want me to report this to the NAACP. So you tell him I will not be back. And for him not to contact me, period." And that was the last of them. I didn't hear from them. I didn't see them.
>
> But you see, just like they do that to me, how many other black women are being mistreated and exploited?

Not being able to receive phone calls and being taped are extreme forms of mistreatment, to be sure. But that domestics, particularly those who live in, are subjected to levels of dehumanization and invasions of privacy unheard of even in other blue-collar occupations is apparent. More than one domestic said she had suspected her employer of searching her room on her day off. (And one employer I interviewed, as we have seen, admitted having done so.) One can understand how Margo Townsend could conclude that "women who hire domestics feel they've bought a slave. She becomes a possession. They don't feel the domestic is a person, that she's human."

Ms. Ryder and Ms. Roy handle their very negative valuation of domestic service in quite different ways. Anne Ryder seems to separate her sense of self—strong and intact—from her assessment of her occupation—low and valueless. Her identity is based on something else (her church activity? her family?), something not apparent from our interview. But this distancing of herself from her job works to keep her self-esteem intact, a mechanism she apparently has used all of her life, evidenced by the fact that she remembered few of her employers' names and "didn't like any of them." Elizabeth Roy translates her anger into action and is one of the two (with May Lund) most politically active domestics I interviewed. She enjoys the travelling and speaking that the proselytizing of her cause entails. Her attention to dress and grooming reflects her awareness of being a somewhat public person. Her negativity and anger, instead of debilitating her, infuse her with energy and caring. No longer the "victim" in the house in Lexington, feeling "unusefulness" to herself, Ms. Roy has taken advantage of opportunities (specifically, the widening job market for black women and a training program for domestics), has moved out of what she considers a "stigmatized" occupation, and has become quite useful to herself and other domestics.

The lives of these five women illustrate quite different experiences in domestic work. Yet the twenty women I interviewed did share some common views and experiences of their work and of employers that recurred so frequently that they deserve mention. First and foremost, all domestics concurred that employers appreciated some forms of deference and outward signs of subservience. As domestics talked in detail about this aspect of the relationship, I came to realize this formed the essence of the employer-domestic relationship. I have, therefore, devoted the subsequent chapter to an exploration of these behaviors and the thinking behind them. At this point, what is noteworthy is that the domestics I interviewed were in agreement that employers liked subservient behavior and did not like a domestic's being too educated or intelligent, too materially well off, or too attractive. Part of being a domestic was acting like the person the employer wanted her domestic to be. The better this performance, the greater the probability of the domestic receiving more than the minimum in material and emotional rewards.

And, like employers, domestics have definite preferences. There were the expected anti-*nouveau riche* remarks, such as Jane Louis' and Lee Evans':

> If the people you work for have money and no culture, forget it. (Ms. Louis)

> I won't work for somebody who just got their two cents together. They don't know what they're doing. They're insecure about their positions. And they don't know how to relate to their help. (Ms. Evans)

This preference for working for higher-class "old money" has been articulated by servants since the nineteenth century, when "new money" first started employing servants in large numbers.

And there was the expected preference for younger women, seen as less prejudiced and less "picky." But it should also be noted that younger women were described as maintaining dirtier houses ("I bring my own lunch; I wouldn't eat anything out of such a filthy kitchen") and as probably going to become "like their mothers" as they grow older.

Elizabeth Roy, May Lund, and Julia Henry were the only domestics who had worked for black employers; and their attitudes toward these situations were similar:

> I definitely prefer working for my own color. Dr. Babcock was real nice. She always complimented me and expressed her gratitude for what I did. That means a lot. And I got very close to her daughter, being there with her all the time. . . . That was the best work situation I ever had. (Ms. Roy)

> We were employer-employee and we were friends. When I was at her house, it was one thing; when we were out socially or in a group, it was another. She had a lot of dinner parties and invited me and my family as guests. We had real respect for one another. She was always home when I worked there and we just worked side by side. We'd go through that house like Grant went through Richmond, then we'd go shopping. That's just

> the kind of person she was. We used to go a lot of places together. We shared confidences. We became real friends. No other employer treated me like that. (Ms. Lund)

> The husband was a professor [at a local college]. They lived in Mattapan. They were very good. I'd like to work for them again if they need somebody. He was a real gentleman and the boys were nice too. You know, I think I'm going to call her and see if she might be looking for somebody. It was really nice there. (Ms. Henry)

Black employers, lacking racism and with a class prejudice modified by the heterogeneity of most black families and a history that has bred a sensitivity to the less fortunate, appear to establish a very different kind of relationship with their black domestics than white employers do perhaps even with their white domestics.

The only other ethnic group singled out by a number of the domestics were Jews. (The areas of Boston to which black domestics have the easiest access by public transportation are areas heavily populated by Jews.) A few shared Esther Jones's view that "Jewish women are the worst to work for. Gripping, complaining, pushing you. But it's the women, not the men." But even those who were critical of the work demands agreed that, on the level of interaction, Jews treated their domestics humanely. Pat Owens', Anne Ryder's and Jane Louis' comments were typical:

> I will not work for nothing but a Jew. Because Jews are very understanding. You have plenty to eat. It's just like home. (Ms. Owens)

> I worked for a Jewish family; she was kind of nice. One thing about the Jewish people, you could talk to them

> just like you talk to anybody else and they wouldn't fire you. But you get with these American people, you couldn't talk to them. (Ms. Ryder)

> I'm partial to Jewish people. I have a nice relationship with them. They're basically more with us. I find Jewish people will help you more if you've got it. They'll give you ideas and help you more. (Ms. Louis)

Finally, domestics, like employers, preferred to work with another woman. The reason given was the risk of sexual advances from male employers. Most domestics were reluctant to expand on brief remarks like, "Men tend to get fresh." My probing for more specifics brought comments like, "Well, a lot of my girlfriends tell me they've had problems with men they worked for." This was an area of discussion that, understandably, caused embarrassment. But the number of oblique statements like Julia Henry's clearly suggested that some of my interviewees had themselves had unpleasant experiences: "And I won't work for any more men. I've tried it a couple of times with these men. They don't seem to act right."

Only activist Elizabeth Roy was willing to describe one such experience which she had had as a nineteen-year-old live-in servant in Alabama:

> The old man was rough. I worked there a while, not too long. The reason I left—they had a bad teenage son who was roguish and mean and I didn't trust him. He *and* the husband made advances. But I didn't report it; I just left. The husband would say what he could do for me if I did certain things for him. Also, the son. They was in my room constantly. They'd come in when the wife would leave. I felt very uneasy. The grandfather was there and

I'd have to say, "If you don't leave, I'm going to call Mr. Johnson."

Margo Townsend recalled an incident in which a young domestic recently from the South came to her (as director of a support and training program for domestics) in the early 1970's complaining of sexual harrassment by the husband of her employer: "So we called this woman, now this is a prominent Bostonian, mind you, and we explained the problem. And you know what she said? 'What do you think I brought her up here for?' I was shocked. We got her out of there, found something else for her." I asked Ms. Townsend how common occurrences of sexual harrassment were among the hundreds of domestics she had had contact with while directing this program. She replied, "It happened to a number of women in our program, mainly to the live-in help. That's why people want to get out!"

Most of the domestics in Ms. Townsend's program were migrants from the South; today, live-in domestics are increasingly immigrants (particularly from the Caribbean and Latin America) and sometimes illegal. The material desperation and precarious status of such women make them especially vulnerable to material and sexual exploitation. While using domestics sexually has never been as pervasive in this country as in nineteenth-century England or contemporary Latin America, my research indicates that this unspoken problem nevertheless does exist and is widespread enough for all of the domestics I interviewed to give it as the reason for now avoiding male employers.

Both employers and domestics stressed the importance of the relationship in this labor arrangement; both expressed a preference, for different reasons to be sure, for working with another woman. Since the employer has more power in the dyad (as well as in the larger society), it is not surprising that the actual relationship reflects her desires more than those of the domestic. What are her desires? How does she want the domestic to act? Why? And how do domestics react to employers' behavioral demands? This chapter has included glimpses of a number of different kinds of relationships. But, as varied as they may be, patterns can be discerned. The following two chapters examine these patterns; they attempt to answer the essential question of this research: what, exactly, is going on between the women?

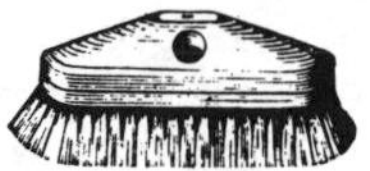

5. Deference and Maternalism

> The baseness of the domestic must not seem to be the result of the airs, contortions or ruses suffered under the yoke. On the contrary, the more the domestic is crushed, the more the master is justified. This is not surprising once one has understood the general phenomenon of the reversal of the accusation in all oppressive relationships.[1]

The relationship between domestics and their employers is extraordinarily multi-dimensional and complex but, at its essence, I will argue, it is one of exploitation. It may appear too obvious to even state that domestic servants have always been an exploited group of workers. But I submit that this labor arrangement goes far beyond the exploitation in the economic sense in which the term is usually used. What makes domestic service as an occupation more profoundly exploitive than other comparable occupations grows out of the precise element that makes it unique: the personal relationship between employer and employee. What might appear to be the basis of a more humane, less alienating work arrangement allows for a level of psychological exploitation unknown in other occupations. The typical employer extracts more than labor. This fact was suggested by the employers' preference for an individual woman over a cleaning service and the numerous statements in which employers made clear that work performance was not their highest priority in evaluating their domestics. The personality of the worker and the kinds of relationships employers were able to establish with them were as or more important considerations. As historian David Katzman has stated, "In domestic employment a personal relationship is part of the job, and the worker is hired not for her labor alone but also for her personality traits."[2]

Why are these aspects so important? And what, exactly, are employers seeking from these relationships? The psychological exploitation of domestics is highly significant for, I submit, it has the two essential functions of affording the employers the self-enhancing satisfactions that emanate from having the presence of an inferior and validating the employers' lifestyle, ideology, and social world, from their familial interrelations to the economically and racially stratified system in which they live.

These aspects of domestic service—these ego and system-supporting psychological functions—as well as the low-cost labor it provides may constitute part of the explanation for its immemorial and ubiquitous world history and its tenacious presence in contemporary American life. And it is in the examination of these dynamics that we can begin to identify the impact this occupation has on the social structure—an impact, I hope to show, fundamentally conservative and reproductive of hierarchical social forms.

Psychological exploitation need not be overtly harsh. It is indeed easily identifiable in deference demands, in the treatment of others as invisible or non-humans, and in the use of them as "windows to exotica." But the exploitation may be just as powerful when it is disguised in maternalism, in gift-giving, and in tolerance for irresponsibility. It is the motivation for and the belief system behind such apparently benevolent gestures that make them, in fact, highly beneficial to the employer at the psychological expense of the domestic.

The psychological exploitation of female domestics by female employers is based in the two dynamics that I contend form the foundation of the relationship between the women: rituals of deference and maternalism. This chapter examines in depth the ideas and forms of behavior that comprise these two multi-faceted dynamics. Throughout this discussion, it should be borne in mind that, while each relationship I encountered was unique and displayed these characteristics to greatly varying degrees, deference and maternalism nevertheless emerged as the salient patterns of the employer-servant relationship.

Deference

Erving Goffman has defined deference as a type of ceremonial activity "which functions as a symbolic means by which appreciation is regularly conveyed to a recipient."[3] Although deference may exist between status equals (called "symmetrical deference"), it is more commonly thought of, and its use in this discussion will be, "as something a subordinate owes to his superordinate."[4] What is important about deferential behavior between non-equals is that it confirms the inequality and each party's position in the relationship to the other. If the superordinate believes the relationship to be unequal, one might ask, why are such behaviors necessary? Because one's consciousness is confirmed only by that of another; one's superior position exists only in relation to another. The inferior other must recognize the superior as such and must exhibit confirming behaviors. To do otherwise is to "disconfirm the selves of the participants" and risk eliciting a negative response from the more powerful superordinate.[5] When the superordinate is an employer who expects elaborate forms of deference, the risk is job loss. The domestics I interviewed fully understood that the deferential performance was an integral part of the job expectations of their work.[6]

Goffman has stated that deference behaviors, as all ceremonial acts, are quite varied in character: they may be linguistic, gestural, spatial, task-embedded (related to the attitude and manner with which the individual performs tasks), or part of the communication structure (who initiates speech, speaks more frequently, receives more attention, et cetera). And deference may take the form of avoidance rituals or presentation rituals.[7]

It was not surprising that I encountered instances of all of the above forms of deference within this highly deferential occupation. Three types of linguistic deference are extremely common: most domestics are called by their first names and are expected to call their employers by their last names; both employers and domestics refer to domestics as "girls," regardless of age; and employers appreciate respectful and deferential terms like "Ma'am."

In the over fifty telephone conversations I had when looking for domestic jobs, all of the women (except one) immediately started calling me by my first name. (The woman who was the one exception asked me what I preferred to be called.) When I asked their names, most gave both (for example, Mary Smith), two gave their husband's names (Mrs. John Smith), and eight gave only their last names (Mrs. Smith). All of the domestics I interviewed reported having been called by their first names. Even the domestic who now introduces herself by her last name is still called by her first name by longtime employers. There were, however, two categories of exceptions to this norm: some of the younger employers encouraged their help to call them by their first names. And a few of the older women who had had a series of domestics had called one or two of them by their last names because "she was a lady-lady type," "she was so much older than me—like a mother," or "she wasn't of an inferior social class or anything." What is particularly noteworthy and relevant to this study is that none of these exceptional cases involved a black domestic; none of the employers I interviewed had called a black domestic by her surname nor had the domestic called her (the employer) by her first name. But the difference in behavior is not based solely on race: every employer who has called a domestic by her last name has called more of her other white domestics by their first names. Apparently, white employers do recognize class differences among their white domestics; it is open to question whether they might recognize such among blacks or whether being a member of an inferior caste is sufficient reason to be viewed and addressed as an inferior. In any case, employers' calling domestics by their first names while being called by their last names is the norm in this occupation.[8]

As is the use of the term "girl" for domestics. Although occasionally an employer referring to a domestic much older than herself would use "woman," far more frequently, regardless of any age difference, employers called domestics "girls." This type of nomenclature, suggesting domestics are not adults, has been a tradition not only in this country but in all parts of the world. What Whisson and Weil have to say about the attitude toward domestics in South Africa has cross-cultural applicability: "The inferiority ascribed to the servant not only pervades her whole identity, it is also inescapable. The ordinary 'girl' grows up to be a lady, the servant remains a 'girl' forever."[9]

How do domestics feel about being called by their first names and being referred to as "girls"? A few seemed indifferent ("No, it doesn't bother me none. That's just what people say") but most, like Odette Harris, disliked such language (a dislike, however, never expressed to employers):

> I didn't like it. Why am I your "girl"? I didn't like it because it sounded like ownership. Like masters and slaves, talking about "my." . . . But you had to accept being called a "girl" and being called by your first name. You would prefer to be addressed as "Miss" but there wasn't anything you could do so you accepted it. . . . They never referred to us a "ladies." They figured it's too nice for us. We're not "ladies."

That employers used "girl" was not unexpected; that domestics used it also was intriguing. My attempts at probing this with domestics yielded little: "Everybody says that": "I don't know. I always say 'girl.'" The explanations that were offered by domestics for their using "girl" for themselves and "lady" and "woman" for employers indicated only that they did it out of habit, conforming to the language use they heard around them. I consider their using these terms an unexamined remnant of what Fanon called the "colonized mind." Language, like other socially constructed systems, usually serves the interests of the powerful. Even when one is conscious of oppressive elements in a language, it is difficult to eliminate them from one's vocabulary. (For example, try avoiding the myriad negative uses of "black" and "dark" that form the foundation of racism in English: blacklist, blackball, the black market, a black heart, a dark day in history, the forces of darkness, a dark mood, et cetera.) The powerless may accept some of the vocabulary and definitions of the dominant society even when degrading and inaccurate; more often than not, however, they retrieve their dignity by altering definitions and operating on the basis of different values.[10]

As stated, in many societies, "childlike" has been applied to domestic servants. But in the West, it has been applied also to women, to the lower classes, and, for the last half-millennium, to people of color. This is not a surprising conceptualization considering the fact that those with the most control over language and ideology were upper-class, male, and white. That much of the subtle and obvious language that has supported this way of thinking has been accepted into the vocabulary of these powerless groups is undeniable; the degree to which they accept the words as describing reality is more questionable. Certainly, in this instance, using "girls" in reference to themselves is an example of such an acceptance of a word but a rejection of its accuracy: these women did not consider themselves, nor did they act, childlike in any way.

Domestics concurred that employers enjoyed being called deferential terms like "ma'am." Recall that Margo Townsend, the director of a social service and training program for domestics, had said this was part of the reason Northern employers preferred Southern black women over Northern: "They would stipulate, 'I want a Southern girl.' They liked the 'Yes, Ma'am' and the 'Yes, Sir.' They *loved* that." May Lund's remarks exemplify those of all the domestics: "Before, I used to 'Yes, Ma'am' and 'Yes, Sir' them to death. No matter how much work they piled on: 'OK, all right.' They just want you to agree."

Were there employers who were exceptions? Domestics said no. A number of my employer interviewees indicated indirectly that they enjoyed such ingratiating language. For example, Holly Woodward, one of the most sensitive and enlightened employers I interviewed, glowed when she described her first encounter with a Jamaican domestic who came to be her favorite of the many she employed in thirty years: "I had been ill and when I came from the hospital, there she was at the door, beaming: 'What can I do to help you, Ma'am?' She was one of the nicest things that ever walked."

My own way of discovering the power of such deferential language was revealing. Although Ms. Caton and I had agreed at our interview that I would start working for her the following week, she called me the night before I was to begin and expressed hesitancy about hiring me because "you seem so well educated." Because I had completed my first set of domestic jobs, I had, in fact, gone to this interview somewhat carelessly relaxed: I carried myself and spoke in a natural way, without the deliberately subservient manner I had feigned during my first set of job interviews (when I questioned if I could successfully pass myself off as a domestic). Because her call caused me concern about retaining the job, I arrived the following day looking especially shabby (baggy slacks, old work shirt, cotton headscarf tied Southern-style) and with an exaggeratedly subservient demeanor (standing less erect, eyes usually averted from hers, a tentativeness of movement). Most important, I said almost nothing, asked the few necessary questions in a soft unassertive voice, and responded to her directions with "Yes, Ma'am." I was rather shocked at her obvious pleasure over and total lack of suspicion about this performance, especially since she had encountered me without it the previous week. To me I felt like an absurd and transparent caricature of Stepin Fetchit; her mind, however, was clearly eased of the apprehensions she had had about my suitability for the job. She did not question the change; my behavior now expressed my belief in my inferiority in relation to her and thus my acceptance of her superiority in relation to me. Her desire for that confirmation from me was apparently strong enough to erase from her memory the contradiction of my previous behavior.

Some of the domestics I interviewed told stories of having been highly successful with what they considered extremely phony and sometimes humorous performances. No employer ever mentioned this directly but, like Holly Woodward above, told stories in which the domestic clearly behaved deferentially. For a few domestics, ingratiation had become a part of their personalities. At issue, however, is not the genuineness of the deference act as an expression of the true feelings of the worker; it is the fact that such behavior is encouraged by employers and exists mainly because of this encouragement.

Closely related to these linguistic forms of deference are those that take place in the structure of communication. Nineteenth-century manuals on the proper demeanor of domestics admonished them not to initiate conversation and to answer as briefly as possible. This was part of the effort to make domestics invisible (about which more will be said in the next chapter), but it was also a way of confirming inequality. Further, it is considered appropriate for mistresses to ask more personal questions than domestics have the right to ask. This is not an uncommon form of ritual between unequals: "Between superordinate and subordinate we may expect to find asymmetrical relations, the superordinate having the right to exercise certain familiarities which the subordinate is not allowed to reciprocate."[11] These kinds of limitations on the speech of domestics are a part of avoidance rituals that exist in all interpersonal communication but take on the quality of imbalance in that between unequals. In all relations, respect for the other's "honor" is expressed through what Simmel calls "discretionary" behavior. Language is one instrument the restrained use of which expresses respect:

> An ideal sphere lies around every human being. Although differing in size . . . according to the person . . . this sphere cannot be penetrated, unless the personality value of the individual is thereby destroyed. A sphere of

> this sort is placed around man by his "honor." Language very poignantly designates an insult to one's honor as "coming too close": the radius of this sphere marks, as it were, the distance whose trespassing by another person insults one's honor.[12]

And the radius of the sphere of privacy is greater the higher the individual on the social scale; or, as Goffman puts it, "the higher the class the more extensive and elaborate are the taboos against contact."[13] By limiting the right to initiate conversation and the amount and content of domestics' speech, employers are in another way confirming their superiority, allocating to themselves the right to greater privacy and greater familiarity toward domestics.

This privilege of familiarity affords the employer another kind of opportunity beyond reinforcing inequality. For many, their contact with their domestic is the closest relationship they have with a lower-class or Third World person. Talking with the domestic is a chance to explore what they assume is a very different lifestyle. The domestics I interviewed reported having been asked "very personal questions"—about their finances, children, marital situations—that clearly had made them uncomfortable. Some dismissed it casually ("They're the biggest gossips in the world!") or felt it came from the women's leading lonely and boring lives. But others felt it was more significant. Nancy Clay said:

> They want to know all your business so they know just where you're coming from. They tell you some of their problems so that you'll tell them your business. It's knowledge for control they want. They're uneasy if they don't know enough about you, if they don't know what you're thinking.

And May Lund attributes it to racial curiosity:

> They've read or heard a lot about black people. They know we've been an oppressed people and they want to know what keeps us going. And they want to know how you handle stress, how you manage to do all you have to do. They want to know your secrets.

However, giving an answer that in some way satisfied the employer was a necessary survival strategy. No domestic reported having told an employer that what she had asked was none of her business or was something about which the domestic did not choose to talk. A few suggested they sometimes fabricated stories ("Oh, I tell her anything") but most said they answered in a way that would both satisfy the employer and protect some of their privacy. It is reasonable to assume, however, that the more powerless the domestic felt, the more she might acquiesce to the mistress' inquisitiveness and actually reveal more about her personal life than she wanted or would later choose to admit to me. Live-in workers, particularly recent migrants and the foreign-born, would be more vulnerable to this type of exploitation because of their precarious positions.

In his 1953 study of blacks in Amherst, David Chaplin, too, discovered that domestic servants "found themselves drawn into a peculiar relationship involving self-abasing exposés of the most intimate details of their private lives as part of a quite unconscious bargain with paternalistic employers. Female domestics were subject to a sort of verbal voyeurism on the part of their mistresses."[14] And he, too, found lies to be sometimes employed to satisfy the mistresses' needs:

> This situation suggested to the servants, consciously or otherwise, the possibility of playing on the sympathy or lurid imagination of their employers by elaborating and often inventing debasing anecdotes about their private

> lives. They were, in effect, catering to the least complimentary elements of the Negro stereotype.[15]

Chaplin's comments lead us to another aspect of this type of "verbal voyeurism." Beyond the fact that by asking such questions the mistresses are asserting that their superior position gives them the right to such intrusive familiarity, beyond displaying a natural curiosity about another person and culture, they may also be looking for titillation and for confirmation of their negative stereotypes about the personal lives of black people. A part of traditional American racist stereotyping is the belief in the less inhibited social and sexual life of black people. This belief reinforces the overall image of black inferiority, since mental activity and self discipline are valued in the Western ethos while sensuality and lack of discipline are disdained.[16] Employers' encouragement of lively stories about domestics' personal lives both satisfies their desire for gossip and, more significantly, confirms their belief in the inferiority of blacks/domestic workers/the lower classes—a belief that is part of the justification of a system that maintains such people in a disadvantaged position. The use of domestics as "windows to exotica," then, is hardly the innocuous interchange it appears to be.

A related, though less prevalent, type of familiarity between the women is employers' using domestics as confidantes. Some domestics heard details of their employers' extramarital affairs; many heard about strains in employers' marriages. In the South, Elizabeth Roy's employer, after sharing the details of the causes and incidents leading to her divorce, told Ms. Roy: "'I've told you things that I wouldn't even tell my mother.' We were friends! When she was in trouble, I was too. When she cried, I cried." Domestics as confidantes are not rare. Former domestic Jane Louis explains it this way:

> Most employers like to talk to the people who work for them because you're not in their circle, you're not going to tell anybody who's important to them. I've been like a confidante. . . . They talk to you anyplace. A white person will go up to a black stranger and tell them very private things—because they know it's not going to go.

Using a domestic as a confidante may, in fact, be evidence of the distance in even the closest of these relationships. Employers can feel free to tell domestics secrets they would not share with their friends or family precisely because the domestic is so far from being socially and psychologically significant to the employer. As physically close as the domestic may be, she is so existentially distant in the mind of the employer that the employer does not even entertain the possibility of the domestic's divulging secrets to those within the employer's social universe. And the employer does not care what the domestic thinks of her for, as Fanon suggested, a person cannot be hurt or insulted by the judgments of those she genuinely believes to be her inferior.

Gestural and task-embedded deference, in the case of domestic servants, may be found in the subservient demeanor and attitude toward tasks. If demeanor is "that element of the individual's ceremonial behavior typically conveyed through deportment, dress, and bearing, which serves to express to those in his immediate presence that he is a person of certain desirable or undesirable qualities,"[17] the subservient demeanor of the domestic servant is expressed not only through her unchallenging stance, her practical and deliberately unattractive clothes, and her controlled speech. She is further asked to convey a certain attitude toward the work: that she is more than willing to undertake assigned tasks and she takes pleasure in serving. Employers not only want work done efficiently, they want domestics to project a particular attitude toward them (the employers) and the work. Some employers, like Frances Stewart and Mary Beck, implied this in their comments:

> I would forgo a lot of efficiency in favor of other factors, partly to have someone pleasant around when you're there. (Ms. Stewart)

> They didn't last long if they came and it was obviously just a job. (Ms. Beck)

But domestics like Lee Evans left no doubt:

> Sure, they still like the Uncle Tom performance, the grinning maid. They eat that up!

Ingratiating behavior has been displayed by many categories of subordinate people because of dominant groups' desire for it. Domestic servants, Afro-Americans, and women are three such groups that have been encouraged to incorporate ingratiation into their encounters with employers, whites, and men, respectively. It was not surprising that a few of the domestics were ingratiating even during our interviews (all older Southern-born women) and many more described having so performed when on their jobs. I watched the personalities of two of the domestics with whom I worked change dramatically when they interacted with their employers and their employers' teenage children. I watched this performance and knew how much it hid. In interacting with employers, these women put on a mask that covered their real selves most effectively. For some domestics, Jacklyn Cock's observation is unquestionably true: "The domestic worker's main mode of adaption is the adoption of a mask of deference as a protective disguise."[18]

Throughout the literature on "Uncle Tomming" runs the debate about the degree to which the person consciously performs without accepting its premises of inferiority or actually comes to believe its premises and thus becomes the role. This debate is a microcosmic version of the discussion among British sociologists about whether there are genuine "deferential workers"—that is, categories of workers who both behave deferentially and accept their subordinate position "as a necessary, acceptable, and even desirable part in a natural system of inequality."[19] Both of these debates entertain the possibility that there may be some groups of people who believe that their own group is innately inferior and is justifiably on the bottom of a legitimately in-egalitarian social system. Both discussions are sophisticated versions of the search for the "happy slave." Empirical efforts to find such "deferential workers" have failed.[20] As they must.

But the "Uncle Tom" *performance* does exist. Is it only because of the encouragement of dominant group members? Hortense Powdermaker has suggested another reason for its existence: it allows members of a subordinate group to express their anger toward their oppressors in a socially acceptable way. "This type of Negro," Powdermaker states, "is conscious of . . . resentments" against whites, and her "meek, humble and unaggressive" demeanor is, in fact, a culturally approved adaptation to a powerless situation. The black who "Uncle Toms" derives pleasure from the performance. This "unaggressive aggressiveness" yields two kinds of psychological rewards: appeasement of guilt and a sense of superiority. If she is a Christian (and all of the domestics I interviewed considered themselves Christians), she believes it is sinful to hate; acting meekly, even lovingly, relieves her of the guilt she feels for these "conscious and unconscious feelings of hostility and aggression toward white people." Additionally, this role may make the domestic feel superior in these ways: hers will be the final victory in the hereafter; she is demonstrating that she is spiritually superior to her employer; and she enjoys the success of being able to fool whites.[21]

Powdermaker contends that such performances on the part of blacks are always deliberate. As one of her respondents stated: "When I'm around them, I act like they are more than I am. I don't think they are, but they do. I hear people say that's the best way to act."[22] My research supports Powdermaker's position: no domestic I interviewed or observed gave any indication she believed herself inferior to her employers. (A few even indicated they considered themselves superior in their more humane value system and in some of their capabilities, particularly childraising.)

Thus, many factors—including the psychological rewards to the domestic, her religious and cultural background, her age and class—might contribute to a domestic's choosing to undertake the "Uncle Tom" performance. But it is important to keep in mind that the main reason such performances exist is because the employers, the more powerful member of these labor dyads, want them. Not as prevalent today as in the past, not as much a part of younger domestics as of older, or of non-Southerners as of Southerners, such deferential behavior nevertheless remains a rewarded if not required, a demeaning if not destructive, element in domestic service. Of this tradition in the racial "etiquette" of this country, James Baldwin writes:

> I have great respect for that unsung army of black men and women who trudged down back lanes and entered back doors, saying "Yes, Sir" and "No, Ma'am.". . . They did not like saying "Yes, Sir," and "No Ma'am" but . . . these black men and women knew that the job had to be done, and they put their pride in their pockets in order to do it. It is very hard to believe that they were in any way inferior to the white men and women who opened those back doors.[23]

Spatial deference takes two main forms in domestic service: the unequal rights of the domestic and the employer to the space around the other's body and the controlling of the domestic's use of house space. The domestic does not initiate touching her employer and is careful to respect the private space around the employer's body by maintaining distance. The respect shown in the honoring of the employer's body space gives a message similar to that given by the domestic's limited use of language: the retention of greater distance suggests that the employer's mental and physical privacy are more valuable and therefore should not be easily intruded upon. Further, rarely does the domestic sit in the presence of the employer (unless on her lunch break). Even when work has stopped for a moment because the two are discussing something (the correct cleaner to use, how to move the furniture to vacuum, what was done inadequately last week, what the high priority tasks for today are) the domestic remains standing. The employer exercises the flexibility she is allowed as the superior and as a woman in her own home: she sometimes sits, sometimes walks around. Both of these conventions affirm the inequality of the relationship and the higher worth of the employer.

Within the house too, there are unarticulated limits on the domestic's movements. Trudier Harris writes insightfully about the relegation of domestics to kitchens:

> The most comfortable realm of [the domestic's] existence is the kitchen; it becomes the black town, the nigger room, of the white house. The black woman cleans the living room or the dining room or the bedroom or the bathroom and retires to the kitchen. . . . The kitchen is . . . the one room in the house where the white woman can give up spatial ownership without compromising herself. Kitchens have connotations of hard

> work and meniality—sweat, grime, broken fingernails, and other things from which the mistress wishes to dissociate herself. Passing *that particular* space on to the domestic is a royal decree of her subservience and inferiority. . . .
>
> Place in any context espouses the hierarchy of masters and slaves, owners and owned, privileged and non-privileged. As an inheritor of this unpleasant tradition, the black woman who works as a domestic . . . knows her place as the whites define it, either the physical location of the kitchen or the status of inferiority.[24]

Harris convincingly argues that the controlled use of house space is another mechanism by which the inequality of the mistress-servant relationship is affirmed.

And controlled use of house space converges with interpersonal spatial deference in eating arrangements, revealing and reinforcing both the domestic's place in the kitchen and the intrafamilial hierarchy of worth. While it is not unusual for an all-day or live-in worker sometimes to have lunch with her female employer in the kitchen, it is practically unknown for the domestic to eat in the dining room and when the husband is present. Marna Houston's eating arrangements with her domestics emphasized house-space deference: "I never had the kids [a series of live-in domestics] eat with us because we eat in the dining room. They'd eat in the kitchen." But Holly Woodward's eating arrangements were deliberately designed to afford her husband, in particular, personal deference: "I'd usually ask them not to come down for breakfast. [The entire family ate breakfast in the kitchen.] They'd eat after we were finished. My husband was funny about that. He didn't want them eating with him." And Frances Stewart's comments were representative of the few employers who were uncomfortable with my questions about eating arrangements. Beginning with a liberal response, she then goes on to describe the actual arrangements:

> Well, it's OK with me if they eat at the table with you. But I would rather they served the food too because that's what they're there for. If they want to sit, well. In the kitchen always, if she had time. In the dining room, never. Normally, she brought the food in and cleared up while we were eating.

Eating arrangements are a part of a whole system of controlled movement of domestics within the house that is used to keep her in her "place." Since the higher the person on the intrafamily hierarchy, the more distant the domestic must remain (that is, she may at times eat with the wife and children but never with the husband), the message of this form of spatial deference is clear: the domestic's "place" is on the bottom. Spatial deference, then—both interpersonal spatial deference and domestics' limited access to various parts of the house—serves, as do other forms of deference, to underline the inferiority of the domestic worker.

Maternalism

In 1960, twenty-one-year-old Odette Harris came to Boston from the Caribbean and immediately went into domestic work because, "you know, in the early 1960's, women couldn't get anything but domestic; no matter how intelligent they were, when they come from the Islands, that's the first thing they have to do." Ms. Harris got a full-time, live-out position with a white family who then lived in Roxbury and would later move to Chestnut Hill. She begins her remarkable story:

> I started work at thirty dollars a week. In 1960 now! I worked from ten A.M. until seven-thirty at night after supper. For thirty dollars! Living out! But, you know, I had a burning desire in my heart; why did I leave my country? My island?
>
> They gave you things like clothes and pieces of furniture. They always like to change things in their house so they give the old things to you. But you never think of how many hours of your days are being spent. She [the forty-five-year-old employer] felt if she gave me things, she wouldn't have to pay too much. . . .
>
> When I left after eight-and-a-half years [in 1969], I was making fifty dollars a week.

The question of why Ms. Harris stayed in this exceptionally low-paying position is answered somewhat as she continues.

> They give you a lot of things. They say you're one of the family and you start believing it. You hear it so much. But inside you, you know there's something missing. She treated me very well, exceptionally well. That's part of the way they keep you. They have no choice because you make life easier for them. They're not losing by giving you "darling" and "sweetheart." They're not losing anything.
>
> But at the time, I didn't have a good relationship with [the relatives I was living with] so I thought it was better to work for them since I was getting a little bit of love there. It did give me a sense of belonging. And I needed that.

Ms. Harris was clearly ambivalent about this "loving" treatment—appreciative and cynical at the same time. The two women came to know much about one another, yet were far from open and honest with one another.

> We never talked about very personal things, really. She didn't like my taste in men. She was always curious; she would ask about my friends. They'd pick me up at night. When I got married, I didn't let her see the man I married because she wouldn't have allowed me to. She wouldn't have like him. And she was right. [Ms. Harris has since divorced her husband.]
>
> She did talk about her marriage. But you can't tell a Jewish woman anything. She's married for life. They are the queen. I saw one thing and she told me another thing. I was shocked.

Though these employers never encouraged Ms. Harris to leave housekeeping, they did compliment her on her abilities and intelligence—compliments, Ms. Harris says now, particularly appreciated because she had grown up being considered "stupid" by her family. The positive words were not lost on Odette Harris:

> But what I did with the time I was there—that house had a beautiful library. Intellectual! That house made you think. I didn't spend any time looking at television. I spent it in books. In the afternoon, when she wasn't home, I looked for what I needed. I could think!

When Ms. Harris enrolled in night school to get a high school diploma, her employers allowed her to leave early two nights a week (cutting her work week down to forty-three-and-a-half hours) and gave even more gifts:

> She gave me everything: clothes, furniture. She was genuinely in love with me because I made life easier for her. And I did feel fondness for her.
>
> After a while, I began to resent what they were doing. They have a way of making you feel a sense of guilt by being overkind to you. But, you see, they were doing so much for me to keep me. And I resented it after a while. She was giving so much both because she wanted to keep me as a housekeeper, but they did love me too. A combination of both. And she needed a friend. She was very depressed. . . . She had never fulfilled her personal self. She had a social work degree but her husband had never allowed her to work. So that's why she wanted to support me and help me with clothes and things while I was in school.

Ms. Harris' ambivalence was matched by that of her employer. While supporting Ms. Harris' academic efforts, the employer planned for her life-long services as a domestic:

> She was planning to build a little house in the back for me and my husband. She said my husband would be her husband's valet. This was before I married! Though she knew I was in school, she wanted me to be her housekeeper forever. She said that after the boys left and got married she hoped I would give them each a day. But I just didn't think my life should be for dustpan and cooking. You see? A good brain could have gone down the drain because she didn't believe I could think.

But Ms. Harris knows her employer's view of her was not that simple. On one of Ms. Harris' visits to her since leaving her employ, this same woman "confessed to me that she knew I wasn't cut out just to use a dustpan and a vacuum cleaner. She told me that! I knew I had more potential. And she knew it too."

What finally angered Ms. Harris most about the situation, however, was neither the low pay nor her employers' expectation that she would remain a servant forever. It was the signs of possessiveness and what she calls "being taken for granted." Her employer, Ms. Bond, insisted upon meeting and assessing Ms. Harris' friends, always referred to Ms. Harris as "my girl" (a term Ms. Harris disliked but never objected to), and, most unusual, used a symbolic gesture of possession characteristic of the old South, replacing Ms. Harris' last name with her own (calling her Odette Bond instead of Odette Harris). Yet even in this extreme assault on Ms. Harris' separate identity, she feels there was a positive element:

> I would get angry when she took me for granted. Like when she would call me by my first name and her last name. I didn't like that. It reminds me of slavery, you know? I didn't want her identity. To her it meant I'm just so belonging to her. I didn't say anything. It was like slavery when everybody was called by their master's name. But she called it to me with a good feeling.

Ms. Harris remained there while completing two years of college. She left to begin a homemaking agency of her own. But, even today, she still visits Ms. Bond regularly and still holds intense and ambivalent feelings about the relationship:

> When I left, it was very hard for her. It was hard for me too. It's hard to leave your mother. But I had to do what was right for myself. . . .

> We were friends. Up to today, she thinks she's taking care of me. She's a hen-type mother and she didn't have a daughter. We're still in contact. I'm going to see her soon. But, you know, it's even painful to visit her. I don't know why. I still feel guilty. . . .
>
> There was a lot of possession and belonging. But there was love too, you know?

Indeed. Love, economic exploitation, respect and disrespect, mutual dependency, intense self-interest, intimacy without genuine communication, mutual protection—all of these elements were contained in this extraordinarily complex relationship. But, at its core, the dynamic around which the relationship pivoted was, I submit, maternalism. Though the maternalism in this stituation was perhaps more raw and explicit than in many such relationships and was perhaps partially defendable because of the age and experience differences between the two women, my research indicates that maternalism remains a basic characteristic of the female employer-female domestic relationship, regardless of the situation, regardless of the ages of the women involved.

What is maternalism? And how does it function in the employer-domestic situation? Obviously, maternalism is related to the historical tradition of paternalism in domestic servitude. Indeed, most writers, even today, characterize the relationship between employer and employee as "paternalistic." This characteristic, it is said, is a carryover from feudalism and is part of what distinguishes domestic service from other blue-collar occupations. At the core of paternalism, let us recall from Chapter 2, is the tradition of patriarchal authority, the two basic elements of which are "piety toward tradition and toward the master."[25] The paternalism of domestic service relates to the employer's obligations of protection and guidance in return for the servant's work, loyalty, and obedience. The historical endurance of the personal relationship between employer and domestic has permitted the preservation of this anachronistic characteristic of paternalism.

One cannot take issue with the essence of this argument. Preceding descriptions by both employers and domestics illustrate that the relationship does retain aspects of its feudal and ancient history. But clearly a modification needs to be made on this widely accepted observation: for the people in my study, as for most of the employer-domestic relationships in the United States, the appropriate term is not "paternalism" but "maternalism."[26] And this change is more than semantic: women, who have been the majority of employers of domestics in the West since the nineteenth century, are in a different structural position than are male employers and have modified the relationship in distinctively feminine ways, thus creating a dynamic similar to but not identical with paternalism.

First, and most fundamentally, the words "paternalism" and "maternalism" are not equivalent in their conceptual or social meanings. If paternalism is indeed part of the tradition of patriarchal authority, an authority that stretched from the household head to the kings and church leaders to God himself, there is no comparable "matriarchal authority" in the West of which maternalism is a part. Paternalism is one aspect of a political-economic-ideological power base, the aspect that relates to the exchange of patriarchal protections for service and loyalty; maternalism, on the other hand, is a concept related to women's supportive intrafamilial roles of nurturing, loving, and attending to affective needs. The very different connotations of these apparently parallel words reflect the distinct gender roles in the social structures of the West.

The importance of the employer's being female in affecting the position, tone, and dynamics of the relationship cannot be overestimated. Though the role of employer is a masculine one, a woman in the position alters the way it is both viewed and executed.

Because of the historical exclusion of middle-class women from the economic sphere, administering the work of the servant may be the only experience the female employer has with administrative activities. Most of the women in my study had been employed outside of the house; in this respect, they were representative of American middle-class white women today. But they are certainly not representative of Western middle-class women over the last century. Industrialism created, along with the proletariat, the "housewife," the women removed from the economic sphere and solely responsible for home and family maintenance.[27] And these new middle-class housewives of the nineteenth century created the market for widespread use of domestic servants. Might the servant have been needed to mitigate against the isolation of such women as well as for practical maintenance? There is little doubt at least that servants provided psychological validation of class differences between the women. Recall Lenore Davidoff's observation:

> The surest way of proving social superiority was to surround oneself with "deference givers"; . . . "with one group, domestic servants, the middle class stood in a very special and intimate relationship: the one fact played an essential part in the defining the identity of the other."[28]

I submit that this remains one of the functions of the domestic servant—the validation of the employer's class status (and thus the hierarchical class system). And I go further: the presence of the deference-giving inferior enhances the employer's self-esteem as an individual, neutralizes some of her resentment as a woman, and, where appropriate, strengthens her sense of self as a white person.

All females share a secondary gender position in the society. The female employer of a domestic has lower social and familial status than her male counterpart. Her knowledge of that, her awareness of the limitations on her options because of that status, and her internalization, to whatever degree, of the legitimacy of her inferiority place her in a different position from the male employer in relation to the domestic.

Both the female employer and the female domestic have been socialized to consider themselves and other women inferior. Additionally, both women know that the female employer is not the ultimate authority in the household. Though the husband of the employer usually plays an indirect role, it may be pivotal. Recall that in every case in which an employer wanted to withhold Social Security tax, it was her husband's decision to do so. And a number of my interviewees described situations in which misunderstandings between the mistress and the domestic were reported to him for resolution.

One might think that the attitude and familial role of younger, more educated women would be quite different from that of the traditional white middle-class wife. But, aside from their career independence, my research suggests that their power relationship with their husbands does not vary as much as one might expect. In no employer's situation (or domestic's either, for that matter) did a husband take major housework responsibility. And numerous vignettes by employers revealed that their husbands retained ultimate authority. For example, twenty-nine-year-old Ph.D. Sylvia Peabody related this story:

> I had wanted to invite Karen to our wedding. [Karen had cleaned for the couple when they were living together.] But Bob didn't want to. He didn't see her as a friend as I did. He said she was an employee and it was inappropriate

> to invite her to the wedding. Their interaction was always less intense. We didn't invite her.

During two interviews with employers (aged thirty and thirty-five), both of whom had graduate degrees, worked, and used their own names, their husbands came into the room. One sat and took part in the discussion; the other had his dinner at a nearby table and occasionally interjected comments. These accidental situations, which I would not have thought to seek out, proved to be highly valuable and revealing. I watched both of these women defer to their husbands' comments, never contradicting or even expanding on his points, and smiling more (at both him and me) than before the men came into the room. I watched these women, who had undoubtedly struggled for their professional "liberation," assume mildly "Uncle Tom" behaviors when relating to their husbands. I left their homes with no question about who had final decision-making power about the circumstances of household help whenever he chose to exercise it. My findings support David Katzman's observations on the role of husbands:

> The initial decision to employ a household worker is sometimes made by the husband—to have his wife assume a more prestigious lifestyle, to release her from what he perceives as household burdens, or to induce her to engage in other activities for his benefit. The wife may initiate the idea of employing a domestic, but the husband may control the decision to do so or not. The wage-hour structure may also be determined by the male head of the household, although he may have no direct contact with (and never even meet) the domestic worker. The conditions of employment often reflect the husband's values and goals as much as the wife's. . . . *The husband of the employing family represents power;* the

> authority to fire, to reduce privileges, to make the work more difficult, etc. [emphasis mine].[29]

Both women's having internalized some belief about their inherent inferiority as women, both knowing there is an external power holding more social status than either of them can ever attain and holding final say over various aspects and even the existence of their arrangements, make their interrelations different from those in which one or both parties is male. The employer might herself be a material and psychological dependent. She has the luxury of identifying with power but she is not the ultimate power. Both she and the domestic know this. The domestic must show deference to an agent of a real power; she must show deference to a second-class power figure for survival. Might the fact that the employer is "inferior" in gender and a pseudo-authority contribute to both women's and the society's low regard for the occupation of domestic servant?

And might the fact that the work is what has traditionally been "women's work" have a similar result? The low regard for this sphere of labor—whether paid or unpaid—has been well documented.[30] The female employer, regardless of the degree to which she may have chosen to buy her way out of it, knows that she is seen as responsible for all household maintenance and that this is devalued work. She perceives the person she hires to do such work as doing *her* work in a way the male employer does not. The domestic is something more than an employee; she is an extension of, a surrogate for, the woman of the house. And she operates in what is increasingly the least prestigious realm of women's activities. This view of the domestic on the part of the employer—as an extension of the more menial part of herself rather than as an autonomous employee—may help to explain why the women tend to see domestic service as a more informal arrangement than other occupations.

And, more important, the employer's low regard for this "women's work" can combine with her own sexism, racism, and class prejudice to further degrade the work and the groups already subordinate in the "three structures of power" in the United States (women, people of color, and the lower classes). For some employers, like Alberta Putnam, it is incongruous to hire a man to do such work: "I would feel uncomfortable with a man in that position. I wouldn't feel right giving him orders like that. I even feel funny asking my husband to clean the dishes." For some, like Holly Woodward's husband, it is incongruous to hire a middle-class person: "Then there was Patricia, a fascinating British girl. Her father was an actor and she wasn't sure what she wanted to do. My husband was against hiring her. He told me, 'You don't want help like that around.'" And it may be assumed that for some employers—particularly in the South, Southwest, and Far West, where the servant population has been almost exclusively black, Mexican-American, Native American, and Asian-American—it is incongruous to hire a white. One can begin to see why the lower-class woman of color, just *because* of this society's sexism, racism, and class prejudice might be psychologically the most desirable "type" for a position of servitude and why being associated with this archetypical "women's work" further degrades her—even, or perhaps especially, in the eyes of her female employer. The employer benefits from the degradation because it underscores the power and advantage (easily interpreted as the rightness) of being white and middle-class.

And the employer simultaneously contributes to the continuation of gender subordination in the society: by hiring another woman to do her work, she solves the problems of the tediousness of housework and (if she is employed) of women having "double duty" in a way that does not challenge patriarchal ideas of appropriate "women's work." None of my interviewees—not the young

Ph.D.'s any more than the older employers who had never worked—was pressuring her husband to take more household responsibility. For these women, the masculist idea that housework is "women's work" remained unchallenged. They were willing to take full advantage of the class and racial inequities generated by this social system to mitigate against their gender disadvantage.

It is clearly significant that the domestic represents the employer in the most devalued area of the employer's activities. If, indeed, she sees the domestic as an extension of herself, it is of her least capable and least "feminine" self. Any identification the employer has with the domestic is a negative identification. The menial, unintelligent, physically strong, irresponsible, weak-charactered servant provides a convenient contrast figure upon whom might be projected those aspects of herself most despised and feared. As stated, for this kind of role, the lower-class black domestic, removed from the employer by class, culture, and color, might be particularly useful.[31]

Another important consequence of both parties' being women is the fact that the success of the arrangement is measured by both more in terms of the quality of the relationship than the practical work aspects. Comments like those of domestic Elizabeth Roy and employer Karen Edwards were common:

> The worst thing that can happen in domestic work is a poor understanding with your employer. A bad relationship makes the work that much harder. That's it; a bad relationship. Then you've really got a hard job. You dread it. (Ms. Roy)

> I want reliability, honesty, niceness. The quality of the work is probably the least important thing. (Ms. Edwards)

That women's value system and morality are different from men's has been demonstrated by a number of writers.[32] Though explanations of this vary, the conclusions are consistent: women are more empathetic, caring, service-oriented, relationship oriented, and concerned with others' feelings. Women "judge themselves in terms of their ability to care" and the "feminine personality comes to define itself in relation and connection to other people."[33] This tendency to emphasize relationships helps explain why many employers and domestics placed a higher value on working with an amiable and pleasant person than on more practical aspects of the work situation. (As would be expected, this attitude was more pervasive with domestics than with employers, and more true of employers who wanted childcare, were not working, or were widowed than those not needing childcare or companionship from the domestic.) But this "caring" and "empathy" that are unquestionably a part of the maternalism from employer to domestic must be scrutinized carefully.

The maternalism dynamic is based on the assumption of a superordinate-subordinate relationship. While maternalism may protect and nurture, it also degrades and insults. The "caring" that is expressed in maternalism might range from an adult-to-child to a human-to-pet kind of caring but, by definition (and by the evidence presented by my data), it is not human-to-equal-human caring. The female employer, with her motherliness and protectiveness and generosity, is expressing in a distinctly feminine way her lack of respect for the domestic as an autonomous, adult employee. While the female employer typically creates a more intimate relationship with a domestic than her male counterpart does, this should not be interpreted as meaning she values the human worth of the domestic any more highly than does the more impersonal male employer. Her ideas about the domestic are not different; her style and her needs are.

And an important part of that "style" emanates from the employer's appreciation for the emphasis women place on the affective aspects of any relationship. These elements are important to her and she knows they are important to the domestic—and she uses that knowledge skillfully. Employer Mary Beck made a classically female statement when she said: "If someone is surly, I might not fire them, but I wouldn't make them feel loved." The female employer knows that her treatment (as distinct from material compensation) of the domestic can be critical in maintaining her as an employee. Recall that this was the main reason Odette Harris stayed in her exceptionally low-paying job for over eight years. Ms. Harris was aware of her employer's manipulation of her: "she treated me very well, exceptionally well. That's part of the way they keep you. They're not losing by giving you 'darling' and 'sweetheart.'" But her own emotional needs outweighed her cynicism about Ms. Bond's motives: "I was getting a little bit of love there. . . . And I needed that." All of the domestics I interviewed stressed the importance of the treatment they received from employers in their job satisfaction. The female employer understands the power of emotional rewarding and punishing in a way that the typical male employer does not, and she knows such rewarding will be more effective with a female employee than with a male. Her use of the emotions to control domestics is another distinct aspect of the maternalistic dynamic.

But the fundamental element of both maternalism and paternalism is, of course, the conceptualization of the domestic as childlike. As we saw earlier, this has been a part of servitude throughout history. The tradition of *patria potestas* in ancient Rome meant the male head of the family was responsible for all those in his household incapable of taking care of themselves—namely, women, children, and servants. This tradition survived in Europe throughout feudalism and into the nineteenth century when full citizenship was withheld from servants because of their "dependent child-like employment."[34]

And such views have not been limited to the West. Research on domestic servitude in India, South Africa, and Latin America indicates that servants' being viewed as children is a cross-cultural phenomenon in the contemporary world.[35] (In Latin America, the number of domestics is so high and this perception of them as irresponsible children so pervasive that one writer has speculated that this view of workers has carried over to other occupations and contaminated management-labor relations throughout the continent.)[36]

My interviewees' statements make it clear that this remains an important part of employers' conceptualizations of domestics. For example, when describing a time when her housecleaner criticized her for working outside the home, Jocelyn Minor said:

> I remember there was a kind of veiled reproach. I said to her, "What will you do after you get married?" She said, "Oh, I'm going to stay home. I believe a wife should stay home after she marries." And I'm quite certain that was meant as a reproach. But I didn't take it seriously. I regarded her as an ignorant child.

How old was she?

> About twenty-two going on ten.

Frances Stewart was even more explicit: "I would get angry with them [the various live-in people] over the sort of things you'd get angry with your kids about. You know, you didn't clean that properly. And I'm surprised you'd do that. Or you said you'd be here and you didn't call. Irresponsibility." Ms. Stewart's help included two women from Ireland, a black woman supporting three children in Alabama, a Nova Scotian woman, a French-Canadian male student—none close to being chronologically children. And yet:

> Most live-in help asks for money. Advances. Or they have to take a trip. It's expected. It comes out of future salary. The same way I would with a kid and his allowance, you know; you do the same thing. If people are going to ask for favors, you treat them like children. You get to that point where you have to make sure they feel responsibility. . . . Somehow people living in your house get to feel like one of the children. That's what I've discovered. Mother and Daddy become Mother and Daddy to the help. . . . I was an authority figure. I knew everything. I was threatening to some, I suppose.

Viewing the domestic as childlike justifies treating her maternalistically. Her acceptance of such treatment "proves" she deserves the treatment, which further justifies the attitude. But it should be kept in mind that the employer has the power in this relationship (enhanced by her greater power by virtue of race and class in the society); the domestic behaves as she must in order to survive. She must accept maternalistic treatment as surely as she must accept being relegated to the kitchen and verbal familiarities that are offensive. These conventions are all very much a "part of the job."

Expressions of maternalism that were related to me included giving gifts, the loaning of money, explaining bills, demanding to meet and approve friends, making business calls for the employee, making travel arrangements for her, and (in the South) interceding on her behalf with the legal system. Because the giving of gifts—especially old clothes—has been an integral part of the domestic service experience all over the world and because it persists today as one of the unique "benefits" of household work, a closer examination of this phenomenon, this ubiquitous expression of maternalism, is considered appropriate.

Ava Pearson's way of operating was typical of employers: "I am an easy person to work for. I'm not hard to get along with and I think that's part of their compensation. But I always gave Alice gifts—old children's clothes, pieces of furniture. And, of course, there was the Christmas bonus." And May Lund's response to such generosity was typical of domestics:

> This woman was always giving me her old size five-and-a-half shoes. I wear an eight! But my mother always said, and she did domestic work for years, she said, "No matter what they give you, you take it because one day they're going to give you something worth having." And I dragged those damned five-and-a-half *double A* shoes home! I'd give them to somebody else or throw them away.

> [Another employer] was always offering me bags of stuff. But if it was something I didn't want, I'd thank her, walk out of there, go around that corner and the first trash can I got to, I'd throw it in. But you take it, whatever they give. When she had a party, the next day she'd give me half dead flowers, soggy salad, and leftover Chinese food. Maybe she thought I was deprived and really needed it. But it was all just more dead weight I had to get rid of. She felt like she was really being nice. She was giving me this and wanted me to have it.

Domestics do, indeed, "take . . . whatever they give"—and not only because it might be useful. Domestics know that gifts, like other expressions of maternalism, *must* be accepted. And, further, as Ellen Samuel points out, they know they must appear grateful . . .

> I didn't want most of that junk. But you have to take it. It's part of the job, makes them feel like they're being so kind to you. And you have to *appear* grateful. That makes them feel good too.

. . . because employers, as Margaret Slater reveals, want to see that gratitude:

> Irene would come on a six-month visa, then go home and come back on another six-month visa. . . . She was a very good worker. The French Canadians enjoy a good reputation as domestics, I think. . . . I gave her many things. [Smiling] I remember she was so grateful one time when I gave her an old refrigerator.

In the past, such items were often given in lieu of wages. Western European servants in aristocratic homes of the seventeenth century, newly freed blacks in the nineteenth-century American South, as well as twentieth-century women involved in the "Bronx slave markets" during the Great Depression were all forced to accept used clothing and leftover food instead of the wages they had expected to be paid.[37] In describing how such "payment in kind" was used with Afro-American servants, domestic Elizabeth Roy unknowingly describes an almost universal phenomenon: "Years ago they would give that in place of money. They knew they could take advantage of our foreparents. Some of them couldn't read and write. They couldn't speak up for themselves. They were afraid they'd lose the job. They'd pay you with leftover food and what have you." Today, these gifts are in addition to wages and that, in itself, raises questions about the custom. Why have employers kept giving articles when it is no longer practically useful to do so? What does it mean to the women who give the gifts? Essentially, why is this custom such an integral part of, so congruent with this particular labor arrangement?

First, we must understand that the exchange of objects between people has social as well as material significance.[38] People reveal their views of themselves and others by how they handle objects—objects having been given meaning by the social group. "Goods are not only economic commodities but vehicles and instruments for realities of another order: influence, power, sympathy, status, emotion."[39] What and how goods are exchanged communicates to the parties involved and to the larger social group who the giver and receiver are and what their relationship to one another and to the community is. The exchange of gifts of approximately equal value has existed in all types of societies. Typically, "gift exchange is covered by the norm of reciprocity. . . . A gift giver will experience discomfort if reciprocity fails to occur; but . . . over-reciprocation will [also] produce disturbance in the original giver."[40] But the gifts involved in domestic service are unusual in two ways: no return is expected by either party and the gifts are almost always second-hand or discarded articles. The fact that material goods—wages and gifts—go in only one direction in the relationship is a clear statement that it is one of inequality. In 1925, Marcel Mauss wrote:

> To give is to show one's superiority, to show that one is something more and higher. . . . To accept without returning or repaying more is to face subordination to become a client and subservient. . . .
>
> The gift not yet repaid debases the man who accepted it, particularly if he did so without thought of return. . . . Charity wounds him who received, and our whole moral effort is directed towards suppressing the unconscious harmful patronage of the rich almoner.[41]

And Whisson and Weil, writing almost half a century later in South Africa, more than agree:

> The giving of unreciprocated gifts places the recipent in the position of a child or a beggar, being too poor, too young or too low in status to be able to participate in the system of exchanges which mark the social boundaries of the donors group. . . . [Employers] give in order to assert their dominance and their possession of their servant.[42]

On some level, the women involved in this one-way gift-giving are aware that it reinforces the inequality of the relationship. It strengthens and provides evidence for the view of the relationship the employer, the initiator of the gifts, prefers—that it is a relationship between a superior and her inferior. For this purpose, it is far more useful than giving a comparable amount in wages. (In fact, raising the wages, another medium of exchange, could threaten to weaken the employer's belief in the inferiority of the domestic; for does not the fact that she will work for low wages help prove her inferiority? "To pay more in cash would be to admit the greater worth of the servant, to give more in kind retains the servant as a dependant whilst reducing his moral worth."[43]) Thus the pervasiveness of gift-giving in domestic service: it, like the many forms of deference demanded and the other manifestations of maternalism, serves to reify the differences between the women—be they in terms of class, race, or human worth.

The use of old, discarded articles strengthens this effect: it is a statement to the servant of what kinds of material goods the employer considers appropriate for her. If "gifts are one of the ways in which the pictures that others have of us in their minds are transmitted,"[44] the employer, in giving old clothes and furniture and leftover food, is transmitting to the servant the employer's perception of the servant as needy, unable to provide adequately for herself, and willing to accept others' devalued goods. That domestics do not perceive themselves this way was clear from my interviews, but the fact that gifts have kept coming (through centuries!) illustrates how much employers want to see them so. "Gift-giving is a way of free associating about the recipient in his presence,"[45] and because domestics have less power, they must appear to be what their employers want them to be—needy and grateful. The response of the domestics I talked with could cause me only partially to accept Barry Schwartz's view that "the acceptance of a present is in fact an acceptance of the giver's ideas as to what one's desires and needs are. Consequently, to accept a gift is to accept (at least in part) an identity, and to reject a gift is to reject a definition of oneself."[46] All of the domestics I interviewed said they accepted the gifts their employers gave them. Most of them clearly did not accept the employers' ideas as to who they were and what their "desires and needs" were. But accepting the gifts and acting grateful were seen as another part of the performance necessary to survive in this particular kind of job, a job clearly as demanding on the social skills and acting ability of the domestic as on her cooking or cleaning competencies.

The use of domestics' first names, calling domestics of all ages "girls," the encouragement of performances of subservience, demands of spatial deference, perceiving domestics as childlike, giving domestics used household articles—all of these conventions of domestic servitude have in common the quality of affirming the employee's inferiority. And this purpose is furthered served by other conventions: the domestic is asked to be inferior in her material conditions, in her intelligence, her appearance and sometimes even her character.

Employers who support domestics' educating themselves out of housework are rare. Recall that even Ms. Bond, who supported Odette Harris' attending night school by giving her time off and gifts, was simultaneously planning to build a small house in back of her own so that

Ms. Harris and her (yet unmet) husband would be the Bonds' servants for the rest of their lives. Only one of my interviewees, the untypical Holly Woodward, articulated a desire to see domestics better themselves: "I preferred someone who said she wanted to go to night school. Indeed, that's what Pam did. After she left us she went into clerical work at [a local community organization]." Another employer, Karen Edwards, was sarcastic and somewhat resentful about her domestic's efforts to improve herself:

> Agnes . . . lasted four years. . . . But then Agnes "got liberated" because of the Civil Rights Movement. She felt she should no longer do domestic work. She went into some kind of training and became a health aide in a nursing home. But it was working fine for me until she got liberated.

Most employers, however, said nothing about domestics' self-improvement. But domestics themselves had plenty to say: employers not only prefer less-educated and poor domestics but resent any evidence of domestics' improving themselves and their conditions and "doing too well." Asha Bell was adamant:

> They definitely want less educated servants. They want you to be able to read and write; they might want you to answer the phone and take a message right. But they don't want you to know *too* much.

And May Lund agreed:

> They prefer uninformed workers. They can take advantage of you more. If you go in there like a professional, then they know they got to go by the rules.
>
> A lot of them want to take advantage. That's why they like to hire a lot of foreigners, they like the very young

> and much older people. They don't like that middle group.

There were numerous occasions during my domestic work experience when my stupidity was assumed. A typical example took place on my first day at a turn-of-the-century house in Chestnut Hill. My field notes read as follows:

> As soon as I hung up my jacket, Mrs. Green led me to the Electrolux vacuum cleaner in the hallway. She explained: "Now, this can be used on wood or rugs just by switching the top piece. No, never mind. I won't confuse you with that. Just use the brush side on everything today." The adjustment she referred to was quite a simple one. It consisted of lifting the attachment off the vacuum tube, turning it 180° and replacing it on the tube. She assumed—because I was a domestic and/or because I was black—that I wouldn't be able to learn this maneuver easily.

Unquestionably, May Lund is correct that less informed workers are more easily controlled and this is part of the reason employers prefer less-educated domestics. But, as she herself recognizes, employers also prefer that domestics are not "doing too well" in other spheres. Ms. Lund, for example, hides from her employers the fact that she owns her own home and has a son at an Ivy League college. Domestics told me stories of workers who drive to within a few blocks of where they work and walk the rest of the way so that their employers won't know they own a car. Elizabeth Roy has never told her employers that her son is in college. And some of my interviewees said that on their jobs they deliberately acted less intelligent than they were. Why? May Lund begins to answer:

> If you have too much education, that brings you up closer to their level and they're threatened by you. They're not going to be comfortable with you.

But why hide your home ownership?

> Some whites feel very threatened by you. They just don't want you up on their level; they want you lower. This is mainly true of the middle- and lower-income-bracket whites. The people with real high incomes don't care what you got or what you're doing. But someone just making it, just across that border in Brookline, just barely got there, they don't want to know you've got a home, a car, and don't let them know you've got kids in college!

Elizabeth Roy's explanation is similar:

> You've got to stay down here [making a low gesture with her hand] and act like you're down there. They might say they have nothing against black people but they still want you in your place.
>
> When you tell them where you're coming from, they can hinder you. And they will. When you keep it to yourself, you're puzzling them. If I said my son was entering college next year, and if I'm working for three women who know one another, they're going to gang up on me. When they get together for bridge or tea, they'll say, "Well, she's doing pretty good, she's putting her son through college. We got to cut her hours; we got to let her go." I always say: don't let them know anything.

In these women's statements are suggestions that the desire for intellectually, educationally, and materially "inferior" domestics goes beyond the issue of manageability. And notice that both women discuss the dynamic in racial rather than occupational terms. Statements like "they're not going to be comfortable with you," "they just don't want you up on their level," and "they still want you in your place" point to a subtler reason behind employers' preference for less capable domestics and, in doing so, help us further qualify the maternalism of servitude.

The purpose of this maternalism is *not* to nurture and enhance growth (as is that, for instance, toward the employer's real children). The main function of the maternalism from employer to domestic is the confirmation of the inferiority of the domestic (and, by extension, her class and racial group). Such inferiority cannot be "outgrown" or overcome with education; to allow for this would be to call into question the innateness of the inferiority. If her inferiority is not innate, then circumstances must have created it, circumstances now being maintained by the employer's minimal compensation for the domestic's work. If her inferiority is not innate, then perhaps all lower-class people and all black people could achieve as middle- and upper-class whites achieve if only their material conditions were different. If her inferiority is not innate, perhaps this system, which maintains categories of people at a disadvantage and others who happen to be born with white skin and/or in the middle class at an advantage, is not justifiable. The domestic must remain ignorant and in poor material conditions; to do otherwise is to threaten the employer's basic beliefs about herself, the people around her, her entire social world.

Domestics were insightful in discussing this dynamic in racial rather than class or occupational terms. They know that the wish to believe in the innate inferiority of blacks runs deeper than the wish to believe in that of lower-class white people and that the idea of black ascendancy is therefore a more disturbing, more threatening one. Such attitudes are a part of all interracial interactions in this country, not just those between employers and their domestics. Elizabeth Roy knows through experience—"They might say they have nothing against black people, but they still want you in your place"—what has been supported, albeit inadvertantly, by empirical evidence.

A study conducted in 1973 of sixty-six white female undergraduate teacher trainees ("young, idealistic teachers, most of whom expressed liberal beliefs"[47]) illustrates that even more liberal whites are more comfortable with blacks whom they consider inferior. Each teacher was assigned to work with four students: one white labelled "gifted," one white labelled "non-gifted," one black labelled "gifted," and one black labelled "non-gifted." (In fact, the four students in each group were equal in academic ability). As expected, the gifted white students received the most attention and the least criticism and the non-gifted whites came second. Unexpected and unexplained by the researchers was the fact that the non-gifted blacks came in third and the gifted blacks last:

> For black students . . . the expectation of giftedness is associated with less positive treatment. . . . *Black students in the gifted group . . . were the recipients of almost all the criticism.* . . . It is the gifted black who *is given the least attention, is the least praised, and the most criticized,* even when comparing him to his non-gifted black counterpart [emphasis mine].[48]

The authors make no attempt to explain why the teachers would react more positively to supposedly less gifted blacks despite the fact that all research on teacher response, including this study, has indicated that more gifted students receive more reinforcement from teachers.[49] What is clear is that this preference for the more able child is overridden by a subtle but pervasive aspect of American racism: whites are more comfortable with less capable blacks. The closer a black comes to being the equal of whites, the more she or he is resented. Even in the position of domestic servant, a position intrinsically inferior to that of the employer, the black woman is asked to further confirm her inferiority by behaving deferentially and by hiding abilities and achievements. And that is not all she is asked to do.

Since women evaluate themselves and are evaluated by the society on the basis of appearance more than men, it is not surprising that this would be an issue in this female-female relationship. However, it is difficult to document. The question of the importance of the domestic's appearance first occurred to me when I was working as a domestic. Not only did I feel no encouragement for grooming and working at attractiveness, but unlike any other type of job I've held, I felt the worse I looked (short of unhygienic), the more my employers liked it. I saw domestics with whom I had worked become far more attractive for church and even for our interviews at their homes. That some of the unattractiveness of their appearance at work was due to the type of labor they had to engage in is indisputable; that some of it might have been to express disrespect for the employer is a reasonable possibility; but I submit that on some level they were aware, as I was, that the female employer preferred the presence of another woman whose appearance, as well as other attributes, was inferior to her own. Trudier Harris reached a similar conclusion from her interviews with Southern domestics and extensive reading of the treatment of domestics in Afro-American literature:

> No maid could expect to keep a job if she appeared for it in her Sunday-go-to-meeting dress or if she arrived for an interview with luscious curls, lipstick, and beautifully manicured nails. The message conveyed by that personal

> fastidiousness would be that the black woman was stepping out of her predetermined place.[50]

The domestic's "place" is below her employer in every way (except, of course, in her capacity for prolonged physical labor). Any hint of competition with the employer must be avoided by the domestic's being clearly non-threatening in all ways, including her physical attractivness.

In this context, too, the black domestic might be highly desirable. The racism that permeates the minds of white Americans includes a belief in the intellectual and moral inferiority of blacks; and the Western aesthetic measures physical beauty by a white, particularly Anglo-Saxon, standard. Adding the dimension of physical blackness (with attributes that deviate markedly from white beauty) to the lower-class, menial position of servitude further confirms the inferiority of the servent vis-à-vis her employer.

And some employers displayed a surprisingly high tolerance for behavior that would have brought immediate dismissal from other types of jobs. I heard stories of employers tolerating regular lateness, poor cleaning, drinking on the job, and even theft.[51] Holly Woodward describes a friend's tolerance of her domestic's stealing and tells us much about the reasons for some toleration:

> One of my friends had a domestic stealing underwear from her regularly. As she described it to me later, I said, "Well, didn't you know that there was something wrong?" The girl was taking her personal belongings, her underwear! I could not imagine why she put up with this. Maybe a sense of distance, that help were creatures from another world. They didn't use their human judgment. I think a lot of it's prejudice, sheer. . . . This thing must be stupid, a lot of it's stereotyping.

And Frances Stewart describes her family's enjoyment of their domestic's regular intoxication:

> Doris drank all the time. I don't think she drank my stuff. Sometimes she was so funny. Even when we'd have guests for dinner, she'd come sailing in. She'd put the vegetable dishes on the table and fly out. [Laughter] And you knew that she'd had six shots of vodka. She was just great. Everybody was hysterical about it. Nobody cared about that.

Because the stealing and drinking supported the negative stereotypes about the lower classes and black people, the presence of such weak-charactered employees benefitted the employers by making them feel superior. Such an employee does more psychologically for her employers than any efficient but dignified domestic ever could.

Just as "it is the anti-Semite who *makes* the Jew"[52] and "it is the racist who creates his inferior,"[53] indeed, it is the mistress with her class and racial preconceptions who creates the obsequious, incompetent servant. And for the same reason. The anti-Semite, the racist, and the mistress (obviously not mutually exclusive categories) want the despised others to exist as they have defined them in order to define their own identity as superiors. To maintain the presence of an inferior is to create a setting for the constant enhancement of one's ego by means of the inevitable comparison.

David Katzman, who has done one of the finest historical books on American servitude, recognizes this attraction to the inferior worker, but offers what I consider an inadequate explanation of the phenomenon:

> Some women (like some men) find fulfillment in exercising power over another woman's life. Rather than seeking an intelligent, resourceful, and independent

> worker, they may want a servant to whom they can feel superior and dominating. Employing a domestic offers them a position of power not otherwise available to housewives.[54]

Employing a domestic to whom one can feel superior offers far more, in my opinion, than "a position of power." And it is largely because of these non-material benefits to employers, I submit, that the occupation has existed in such diverse stratified social systems throughout the world. The presence of the "inferior" domestic, an inferiority evidenced by the performance she is encouraged to execute and her acceptance of demeaning treatment, offers the employer justification for materially exploiting the domestic, ego enhancement as an individual, and a strengthening of the employer's class and racial identities. Even more important, such a presence supports the idea of unequal human worth: it suggests that there might be categories of people (the lower classes, people of color) who are inherently inferior to others (middle and upper classes, whites). And this idea provides ideological justification for a social system that institutionalizes inequality.

This ideological function of domestic servitude is part of what has made this occupation a profoundly conservative element in the varied hierarchical societies in which it has existed. This ideological function—based in rituals of deference and maternalism that are as integral to this occupation as are low pay and low prestige—cannot be overestimated in its importance to the perpetuation of the occupation and the perpetuation of a social system of class, racial, and gender stratification.

6. Invisibility, Consciousness of the Other, *Ressentiment*

Invisibility

My field notes from my first day cleaning a large house in West Newton describe this scene:

> Mrs. Thomas and I were both cleaning in her large kitchen when her sixteen-year-old came in to make a sandwich for lunch. They talked openly as if I weren't there—about where he had gone the night before, who he had seen and how angry his father was about his staying out too late. I was surprised at how much rather personal information they exposed. During their conversation, he asked her if cats took vitamins. (The family

> recently got a kitten.) She answered she didn't know but she didn't think so. Despite the fact that I knew there were vitamins for cats, I said nothing because I felt that that was what was expected of me. This situation was the most peculiar feeling of the day: being there and not being there. Unlike a third person who chose not to take part in a conversation, I knew I was not expected to take part. I wouldn't speak and was related to as if I wouldn't hear. Very peculiar.

At a spacious house in Belmont where I worked a full eight-hour day during December and January (when the temperature was regularly below freezing), the psychiatrist husband and his non-working wife usually left the house in mid-morning and returned in the late afternoon. My notes from the first day describe a pattern that would be repeated every time they left the house:

> About a half an hour after they left, I noticed the house getting cooler. The temperature continued to drop to, I would guess, 50°–55°—not comfortable even with my activity. I realized that they had turned the heat down as if there were no one there! I looked for a thermostat but couldn't find it. Worked in that temperature until 5:00 when I left.

And at a more humble ranch home in Needham, where I cleaned half a day each week for a retired accountant and his wife, this event took place:

> They left around 9:30 to make a doctor's appointment for her at 10:00. About forty-five minutes after they had left, the doorbell rang. When I went to open it, I was unable to. I could see through a small circular window in the middle of the door that it was a man delivering a

> plant. I gestured for him to leave it outside. I remembered that Mrs. Brown had always unlocked the door from the inside when I arrived, so I started a futile search for the key. I realized that when leaving the house, they must have locked it as they would when leaving it empty and that the only way I could get out would be to climb through a window. When they returned, I explained why the plant was sitting outside. He laughed and said, "Oh, I hadn't thought about that. You couldn't get out, could you?"

Similar kinds of incidents in which I felt I was treated as though I were not really there happened repeatedly during my seven months of domestic work. On one occasion, while sitting in a kitchen having my lunch while a couple walked and talked around me, my sense of being invisible was so great that I took out paper and started writing field notes. I wrote for about ten minutes, finished my lunch, and went back to work. They showed no evidence of having seen their domestic doing anything unusual; actually, they showed no evidence of having seen their domestic at all. (As Ralph Ellison has observed, "it is sometimes advantageous to be unseen."[1])

But such incidents were always disconcerting. It was this aspect of servitude I found to be one of the strongest affronts to my dignity as a human being. To Mrs. Thomas and her son, I became invisible; their conversation was as private with me, the black servant, in the room as it would have been with no one in the room. For the couples in Belmont and Needham, leaving me in the house was exactly the same as leaving the house empty. These gestures of ignoring my presence were not, I think, intended as insults; they were expressions of the employers' ability to annihilate the humanness and even, at times, the very existence of me, a servant and a black woman. Fanon articulates my reaction concisely: "A feeling of inferiority? No, a feeling of nonexistence."[2]

The servant position is not the only "non-person" role, but, as Erving Goffman has suggested, it may well be "the classic type of non-person in our society. . . . In certain ways [s]he is defined by both performers and audience as someone who isn't there."[3] Other categories of people sometimes treated as though they were not present include the very young, the very old and the sick. What is important about all of these groups of people is that their non-person role relates to their subordination and carries with it some disrespect. Thus the servant as non-person is a perfect fit: the position is subordinate by definition, the person in it disrespected by centuries of tradition.

It has been suggested that it was during the nineteenth century that Europeans began to consider their servants as non-persons.[4] Clearly invisibility was a desirable quality in an American domestic by the late nineteenth century. Writing about this period, David Katzman states:

> One peculiar and most degrading aspect of domestic service was the requisite of invisibility. The ideal servant as servant (as opposed to servant as a status symbol for the employer) would be invisible and silent, responsive to demands but deaf to gossip, household chatter, and conflicts, attentive to the needs of mistress and master but blind to their faults, sensitive to the moods and whims of those around them but undemanding of family warmth, love and security. Only blacks could be invisible people in white homes.[5]

Thus Katzman leads us to the other, race-related, dimension of invisibility: blacks (and, I would submit, all people of color) are more easily perceived by whites as invisible or non-human than are other whites. This is an aspect of racism that has been discussed by many writers. Ralph Ellison wrote of white America's inability to see blacks because of "a matter of the construction of the inner eye, those eyes with which they look through their physical eyes upon reality." For James Baldwin, the "inner eye" of white America is constructed in such a way that despite an Afro-American presence of over four hundred years, the nation "is still unable to recognize [the black person] as a human being." From his examination of the treatment of Third World people in films, Asian scholar Tom Engelhardt concluded that such films promote "the overwhelmingly present theme of the nonhumanness of the nonwhite," thus perpetuating that idea in the minds of the viewing audience.[6]

Even observers of interracial relations in the overseas colonies have pointed to dehumanization as fundamental to such relations. Albert Memmi explained how this mechanism facilitated the control of the colonized Arabs by the French: "What is left of the colonized at the end of this stubborn effort to dehumanize him? . . . He is hardly a human being . . . [and]one does not have a serious obligation toward an animal or an object."[7] But Frantz Fanon, writing of the same colonial dynamic, added the important point that the conceptualizations of those of the more powerful group create reality only for themselves and not for the people they choose to define as other than human.

> At times this Manicheism goes to its logical conclusion and dehumanizes the native, or to speak plainly, it turns him into an animal. . . . The native knows all this, and laughs to himself every time he spots an allusion to the animal world in the other's words. For he knows that he is not an animal. . . . [During decolonization] the "thing" which has been colonized becomes man during the same process by which it frees itself.[8]

Have I gone too far? Are the conceptual leaps from the mistress ignoring the presence of her servant to Asians being portrayed as non-humans in films to the colonizer treating the colonized as an animal or an object too great? I think not. I submit that all of these behaviors are manifestations of similar mental processes. What all of these writers are describing is the reality that, having been socialized into cultures that define people of color as worth less than whites and having observed material evidence that seems to corroborate this view of them as inferior, whites (particularly those in societies with large Third World populations) do, to varying degrees, devalue the personhood of such people. This devaluation can range from the perception of the persons as fully human but inferior to conceptualizing of them as subhuman (Fanon's colonized "animal") to the extreme of not seeing a being at all. And though this mechanism is functioning at all times when whites and people of color interact in this society, it takes on an exaggerated form when the person of color also holds a low-status occupational and gender position—an unfortunate convergence of statuses for the black female domestic servant.

Consciousness of the Other

Yet the domestics I interviewed appeared to have retained a remarkable sense of self-worth. Like the colonized described by Fanon, domestics skillfully deflect these psychological attacks on their personhood, their adulthood, their dignity, these attempts to lure them into accepting employers' definitions of them as inferior. How do they do it? How do they cope with demands for deference, with maternalism, with being treated like non-persons? It seemed to me that their most powerful protections against such treatment were their intimate knowledge of the realities of employers' lives, their understanding of the meaning of class and race in this country, and their value system, which measures an individual's worth less by material success than by "the kind of person you are," by the quality of one's interpersonal relationships and by one's standing in the community.

Domestics were able to describe in precise detail the personalities, habits, moods, and tastes of the women they had worked for. (The descriptions employers gave were, by comparison, less complex and insightful—not, it seemed to me, because employers were any less capable of analyzing personalities but rather because they had less need to study the nuances of their domestics.) Domestics' highly developed observational skills may grow out of the need for maneuvering and for indirect manipulation in this occupation, but the resulting knowledge and understanding is critically beneficial to their maintenance of their sense of self worth vis à vis their employers. Domestics' answers to my questions about their feeling jealousy about their employers' better material conditions gave insight into not only their assessments of their employers but also their value system. Elizabeth Roy's, Ellen Samuel's, and Joan Fox's answers were particularly revealing:

> I used to feel envy of all the things they have. When I was younger, I did have a little envy. I wondered why they could have it all and we didn't have any. But I don't anymore because as I got older and took a good look at them, I realize material gains don't necessarily mean you're happy. And most of those women aren't happy, you know. I feel like I've done a good job. All three of my children came here to me to Boston. They're doing well. I'm proud of what I've done. I don't have any regrets. (Ms. Roy)

> Even today—and he's [her employer's son] a big doctor now—you know, when she wants to tell him something important, she calls me and asks me to call him. 'Cause he'll hang up on her! He hates her! When I was there [when the son was a teenager] he used to yell at her. He never yelled at me. Said then and he says now that I'm more of a mother to him than she is. I still get a birthday card and a Mother's Day card from him every year. Never sends her one. Now isn't that an awful way to live? (Ms. Samuel)

> I wouldn't want to be in her place. She's got nothing to do with herself. The older ones are the worst off. Just go to the hairdresser, go to this meeting, sit around. If you look close, you see they're very lonely. I would never want to stop working, for one thing, even if I could. I would never want to live like that, sitting around, talking foolishness, and doing nothing. (Ms. Fox)

Working in the most private sphere of their employers' lives, domestics see their human frailities and problems. Sometimes employers volunteer the information. I was surprised by the revealing frankness of one of my employers (a Wellesley mother of two small children) the first day I worked for her. My field notes read:

> While I had my tea and she puttered in the dining area, she talked about her switch to health foods and her husband's still eating junk food. For example his breakfast, she said, is usually a Coke and a Baby Ruth bar. I commented lightly that that must be hard for a person into health foods to live with and she said, quietly and seriously, "You learn to live with it. If you want your children to have a father, you have to." She looked

> blankly at the wall as she spoke and when she realized that I was looking at her (with my surprise at her frankness probably showing), she nervously and quickly moved out of the room. I think she had revealed more about marital discontent to the stranger who'd come in to clean than she'd intended to.

And sometimes domestics just observe the contradiction between what employers want to present to the public and what the reality is. (Recall Odette Harris' comment: "I saw one thing [about her marriage] and she told me another thing. I was shocked.")

Thus, domestics' stronger consciousness of the Other functions not only to help them survive in the occupation but also to maintain their self respect. The worker in the home has a level of knowledge about familial and personal problems that few outsiders do. It is not surprising that domestic workers do not take the insulting attitudes and judgments of employers seriously; they are in a position to make scathing judgments of their own. Regrettably, some of the best evidence of their evaluation of their employers cannot be captured in print: it was the cynicism and humor displayed in their derisive imitations of their employers. Raising their voices to little girl pitch, adding hand and facial gestures suggesting confusion and immaturity, my interviewees would act out scenes from their past experiences—typically scenes in which the employer was unable to cope with some problem and had to rely on the guidance and pragmatic efficiency of the domestic. It was interesting that these domestics, described historically and by some of the employers interviewed as childlike, perceived their employers as "flighty" and childlike. How *could* they buy into the evaluations of women they so perceived? When I asked a group of six domestics if they felt like "one of the family" when they heard themselves referred to as such, they laughed in agreement with Elizabeth Roy's cynical answer: "No! Of course not! [Employers] just say that in order to get more work out of you. It's just like that old Southern terminology: 'She's a good old nigger. That's my nigger. I just don't know what I'm going to do without that nigger.'"

The domestics I interviewed knew the importance of knowledge of the powerful to those without power. This significant element in relationships of domination has been discussed by writers as diverse as Nietzsche, Hegel, and Fanon.[9] Nietzsche was extreme in his view that the "slave" is a dependent lacking originality and genuine creativity.

> Slave ethics . . . begins by saying *no* to an "outside", an "other", a non-self, and that *no* is its creative act. This reversal of direction of the evaluating look, this invariable looking outward instead of inward, is a fundamental feature of rancor. Slave ethics requires for its inception a sphere different from and hostile to its own. Physiologically speaking, it requires an outside stimulus in order to act at all; all its action is reaction.[10]

Likewise Fanon, in his early writings, considered the consciousness of the colonized to be totally dependent. Colonized people, he said, "have no inherent values of their own, they are always contingent on the presence of the Other. . . . Everything that [he] does is done for the Other because it is the Other who corroborates him in his search for self-validation."[11] And at the beginning of his famous discussion of "Lordship and Bondage," Hegel appears to agree: "The one is independent, and its essential nature is to be for itself; the other is dependent, and its essence is life or existence for another. The former is the Master, or Lord, the latter the Bondsman."[12]

Domestics have been perceived as a dependent labor group in the past and, in some parts of the world, even today. (In fact, Memmi states that this is the reason servants are the only poor who have always been despised by other poor.[13]) Unquestionably, material dependence has characterized this occupation throughout time; in only a few parts of the world have the labor options of low-income women weakened this material dependence. But I suspect that the psychological independence displayed by the women I interviewed has also existed, to varying degrees, throughout time. Hegel and Fanon both recognized this as a countervailing energy within the apparent dependence—an energy, for Hegel, that developed out of the slave's labor and its effects on his or her consciousness:

> Through work and labour, however, this consciousness of the bondsman comes to itself. . . . Labour is desire restrained and checked, evanescence delayed and postponed. . . . The consciousness that toils and serves accordingly attains by this means the direct apprehension of that independent being as itself. . . . Thus precisely in labour where there seems to be merely some outsider's mind and ideas involved, the bondsman becomes aware, through this re-discovery of himself by himself, or having and being a "mind of his own."[14]

The master, on the other hand, because of his desire-and-consumption pattern of activity, becomes weaker in skills, self-discipline, and overall human development. "It is not an independent, but rather a dependent consciousness that he has achieved."[15] Fanon, too, later recognized the existence of inner-directedness and the importance of tradition in shaping the colonized's thoughts and behaviors. However, Fanon maintained his view that the extensive control exercised by the European colonizer forced the colonized to be in a state of constant awareness when among the colonizers: "The native is always on the alert. . . . The native and the underdeveloped man are today political animals in the most universal sense of the word. . . . The emotional sensitivity of the native is kept on the surface of his skin like an open sore."[16] This view of the powerless as exhibiting the elements of dependence and independence and always acutely aware of the powerful is consistent with the information my interviews yielded. While domestics were indeed "invariably looking outward," carefully scrutinizing the personality, habits, and moods of their employers, they were also inner-directed, creative, and, like Hegel's slave, "having and being a 'mind of [their] own.'"

Domestics, indeed, know the Other. And domestics know the meaning of their own lives. They know they have held down jobs typically since they were teenagers; they know they had the strength to move *alone* from the country or the South or the Islands in order to better themselves; they know they can successfully maneuver in black and white, working and middle-class worlds; they know they are respected by their neighbors for being able to maintain a regular job in a community plagued by unemployment, for their position in the church or the Eastern Star or the Elks, and, most important, for raising good children. Domestics also know the limitations placed on them in this country because of their class and race in a way employers do not, because they need not, know. And they know they have survived and transcended obstacles their employers could not imagine. Free of illusions about equal social opportunity, domestics neither blame themselves for their subordinate economic position nor credit their female employers' superordinate position to any innate superiority of theirs. This ability to assess their employers' and their own lives based on an understanding of social realities and on a distinct moral system is what gives domestics the strength to be able to accept what is beneficial to them in their employers' treatment while not being profoundly damaged by the negative conceptualizations on which such treatment is based. (Recall Odette Harris, who put herself through high school and two years of college while taking from her exceptionally low-paid domestic job what she needed: "I was getting a little bit of love there. . . . And I needed that.") And the fact that all the domestics I interviewed who had worked in both the North and the South said they preferred Southern white women as employers further attests to this extraordinary "filtering" ability.

It may be assumed that most Southern white women are more conservative politically than most Northern white women. Certainly, on the group level, the Northerner's "aversive" racism would be less obviously oppressive than the Southerner's "dominant" style.[17] Yet, the Southern white woman's style of relating to the domestic worker was preferred.

Eleanor Preston-Whyte encountered a similar phenomenon in two sections of Durban, South Africa.[18] Relationships between servants and their employers were far more intimate, familiar, and maternalistic in the lower-income, more politically conservative area than in the higher-income, politically liberal neighborhood. Preston-Whyte attributed the familiarity in the low-income homes to the physical closeness of the women (because of small houses), the more informal family interaction style, which carried over into relationships with servants, and more cultural and experiential similiarities between the low-income employers (frequently of rural backgrounds) and their servants. In the higher income areas

> it was not only culture which divided them but social class, experience and ambition. In the lower-income area, on the other hand, the white and African women may be said to have shared something of common social environment. They could appreciate the other's problems and offered each other genuine sympathy in times of crisis and insecurity.[19]

The apparent paradox of the conservative, apartheid-favoring white who permits intimacy in her home with her servant is explained by

> the very clear acceptance of both parties of the inferior position of the employee. . . . If the groups to which individuals belong are clearly differentiated and unequal to each other, the closest contact may not only be allowed, but it may even be thought fitting. . . . In South Africa . . . close contact between employer and servant may occur at certain levels since it is thought impossible for a relationship of equality to exist between Black and white. There is thus no need for the employer "to keep his or her distance."[20]

Similarly in the American South where, until recently, racial segregation and domination were firmly embedded, the social distance between mistresses and servants, between blacks and whites, was unquestioned. Katzman states that, "since individual white action could not affect the subordinate role of blacks—Southern racial etiquette ensured this—whites could develop a far greater intimacy with their black servants than could mistresses in the North with their servants."[21] Additionally, as in Preston-Whyte's low-income area, Southern white and black women share a great deal in common culturally, certainly more than do Northern white employers and Southern black domestics. Katzman considered this to be one of the differences between the North and the South around the turn of the century:

> For all the differences between black and white in the South, they had in common Southern cultural traditions. The cultural differences between whites and blacks in the South were far fewer than the dissimilarities

> between native-born white mistresses in the North and their immigrant or black servants.[22]

And recall that many of my interviewees had worked in the South for blue-collar families (factory workers, small farmers). Because of the availability of a large cheap servant pool, Southerners of fairly low incomes—that is, with incomes close to that of their servants—can afford household help. One Southern-born domestic referred to the two groups as "co-related":

> There's quite a difference [between Northern and Southern white women employers]. From the Southern point of view, we're kind of co-related, you know. I say "co-related" meaning the Southern black and the Southern white understand each other—whether they like one another or not. You understand their goings and comings. And you feel a little easier with them. And they understand us more than Northern whites do. And treat us better.

Closer in class and culture, operating within a clearly defined system of social and racial inequality, sharing an acceptance of maternalistic behaviors as a necessary and appropriate element of domestic service, Southern black and white women developed a kind of mistress-servant relationship that was psychologically satisfying, to some degree, to both groups of women. Northern employers, on the other hand, operating in communities with unclear rules of race relations, typically having had less experience with blacks than their Southern counterparts, administering to an employee different not only in color but in culture and class, had to struggle to create rules to define domestics' proper place in their homes and psyches. If the Northern employer was also new to the role, the struggle was one of creating both class and racial distance. In any case, this need to create the behavioral norms of racism, since they were not given to Northern employers ready-made as in the South, is part of the explanation for Northerners' treating domestics more coldly. I interpret my interviewees' preference for Southern employers as an expression of both their comfort with the familiar and their desire for a more personal kind of relationship in their work situation—typically a high value, as stated, for all women. Like Odette Harris in her situation in Boston, these women were able to accept and benefit from the supportive elements in Southern maternalism while at the same time rejecting the destructive belief system on which such behavior was based.

Lack of Identification

One might expect domestics' keen consciousness of employers to lead to their identifying with them. Certainly, the characterization of domestics as inevitably identifying with their mistresses is a prevalent theme in the literature on servitude throughout the world. From the upper-level servants of eighteenth-century England to the house slaves of the American South, identification has been seen as a characteristic of this occupation which brings the worker into such constant and intimate contact with the employer.

But identification is, of course, not unique to servitude. The phenomenon is a mode of coping with a situation of powerlessness that precludes overt attack against those with power. By identifying with the persons in power, one is permitted "a vicarious sharing of some of his or her strength."[23] However, this coping mechanism has the unhealthy elements of self-delusion and an admiration for one's oppressor. Bruno Bettelheim discerned it among some Nazi concentration camp prisoners:

> When a prisoner had reached the final stage of adjustment to the camp situation, he had changed his personality so as to accept various values of the SS as his own . . . from copying the verbal aggressions of the SS to copying its form of bodily aggressions. . . . They would try to acquire old pieces of SS uniforms . . . [because] . . . the old prisoners admitted that they loved to look like the guards. . . . [They] accepted Nazi goals and values, too, even when these seemed opposed to their own interests.[24]

But Bettelheim added this significant observation: "These same old prisoners who identified with the SS defied it at other moments, demonstrating extraordinary courage in doing so."[25]

Likewise, writers have discussed such identification on the part of the colonized toward the colonizer. Unlike in the concentration camp, the identification in this situation is a result of direct efforts on the part of the dominant group: the culture of the colonizer is forced upon the colonized through institutions such as the educational and religious. Fanon observed:

> There is always identification with the victor. . . . The black schoolboy in the Antilles, who in his lessons is forever talking about "our ancestors, the Gauls", identifies himself with the explorer, the bringer of civilization, the white man who carries truth to savages—an all-white truth. There is identification—that is, the young Negro subjectively adopts a white man's attitude.[26]

And writers on the antebellum South, like Jessie Parkhurst and Eugene Genovese, have also commented on the identification of house slaves with their owners. But, like

Bettelheim, Genovese sees that this identification had its limits: "On occasion . . . a servant decided he or she had had enough and murdered the white family."[27] What the concentration camp, the colonial situation, and house slavery have in common is the extreme dominance of one group over another and sufficient contact between members of the two groups for those in the less powerful position to have enough knowledge of the ideas and behaviors of the powerful to be able to adopt them to some degree. The existence of contact is critical; it explains why field slaves or the less assimilated colonized are less likely to identify. And it suggests why domestic servants, more than other blue-collar workers, might identify with their employers.

Undoubtedly, servants' identifying with their employers has existed in recent history. Identification may still exist to some degree in the American South and Far West, where servants are less sophisticated and dependency more encouraged. It may even exist in the Northeast among some live-in workers. But the women I interviewed expressed no hint of it. A discussion of the phenomenon was considered appropriate because so many writers have associated it with domestic service and because, frankly, I expected to encounter it. Rather, the domestics I interviewed see themselves, their lifestyles, their values, as distinct from and, in some ways, superior to that of their employers.[28] The closest phenomenon to identification I could discern, and it is quite distinct to be sure, was the extreme consciousness of the Other. As stated, domestics as a group were far more aware of and concerned with the subtleties of personality and habits of their employers than vice versa. But this awareness was that of a distant and somewhat judgmental observer, fully cognizant of her disadvantaged position in the relationship and the society, and conscious that the greater her understanding of those wielding power over her life the greater her potential for maneuvering skillfully and profitably within the employer's world. It was the keen awareness of one who knows that knowledge is power, not the envious and hungry stare of the sycophant. Powerlessness necessitates a state of acute awareness and a stance ready to react; these qualities are not, however, synonymous with identification.

Today's domestic (or at least, the American-born woman in the Northeast), fully aware of an egalitarian philosophy of human worth and opportunity, more psychologically and materially independent than her predecessors (and less fortunate segments of the contemporary pool), defines herself by her family, her church, her organizations, her place in her community. She neither buys into the employer's definition of her nor does she base her own definition of herself on her work situation. Like other blue-collar workers who consider their "real" lives that part that is away from their jobs, domestics' "real" identities come from other than work-related activities. But while the domestics of today are, in fact, more psychologically and materially independent than domestics of the past, they are nevertheless still asked for some semblance of the traditional subservient performance, a performance, it is clear, far removed from their view of their real selves. It is this contradiction of contemporary American servitude that explains why the women I interviewed exhibited such a high degree of *ressentiment*.

Ressentiment

Ressentiment, a French term adopted by Nietzsche into the German language and later thoroughly explored by Max Scheler, denotes

> an attitude which arises from a cumulative repression of feelings of hatred, revenge, envy and the like. . . . When

> a person is unable to release these feelings against the persons or group evoking them, thus developing a sense of impotence, and when these feelings are continuously re-experienced over time, then *ressentiment* arises.[29]

> *Ressentiment* can only arise if these emotions are particularly powerful and yet must be suppressed because they are coupled with the feeling that one is unable to act them out—either because of weakness, physical or mental, or fear. Through its very origin, *ressentiment* is therefore chiefly confined to those who serve and are dominated at the moment.[30]

A critical element of *ressentiment* is the sense of injustice based on the belief that one does not deserve to be in the subordinate position. It is not surprising, then, that *ressentiment* would be "strongest in a society like ours, where approximately equal rights (political and otherwise) or formal social equality, publicly recognized, go hand in hand with wide factual differences in power, property, and education."[31]

Scheler felt that certain positions within a social structure were especially prone to produce *ressentiment*-filled people: the feminine role (especially the spinster), the mother-in-law, and the priest, for example. Individuals in these positions have a sense of deprivation relative to others' power or benefits, with no opportunity to express the anger and envy caused by the deprivation. Clearly, domestic servants are in a similar type of position; they may be, in fact, the epitome of "those who serve and are dominated." And to the degree that they do not believe in their inferiority and therefore see their situation as unjust, they too should feel *ressentiment*. And, indeed, they do.

Despite domestics' knowledge that material comforts do not bring happiness and their assessments of themselves by other than job-related criteria, their awareness of employers' unearned privileges in the society (because of their class and race) and their having to endure employers' demeaning treatment cause feelings of *ressentiment* in even the most positive domestics. Many writers on servitude, from Lewis Coser to Jean Genet, have commented on the hostility that must exist in those who serve.[32] But *ressentiment* is more than hostility; it is a long-term, seething, deep-rooted negative feeling toward those whom one feels unjustly have power or an advantage over one's life. A domestic illustrates her *ressentiment* while describing her "kind" employer:

> She was the kind of person who made up for their dullness by a great show of pride, and she got every bit of her "Yes, Ma'am, Miss Annes" from each and everybody. Since she was that kind of person, I used to see if I could feed her enough of that to choke her. . . . She was, by white standards, a kind person, but by our standards she was not a person at all.[33]

Domestics know that employers have had the power to make the relationship mainly what they want it to be. Domestics may reject the degrading ideas behind the demanded "games," but, like Elizabeth Roy, they also know they have little choice but to play: "Domination. That's the name of the game. The more you know, the more you make the employer uneasy. . . . They want to dominate, exploit." If domestics do not pretend to be unintelligent, subservient, and content with their positions, they know the position could be lost. Esther Jones expresses an understanding all domestics share: "She always said I was one of the family, but I knew better. I knew just what was going on and how they could change. If you don't do the way they want, they'll change overnight!"

Thus, part of their *ressentiment* is caused by the psychological exploitation that my research indicates is intrinsic to this work relationship and part of it is caused by domestics' knowledge of how employers have used their power to also exploit them materially. For domestics are aware of this simple fact: if employers paid better, the quality of their (domestics') lives would be better. Even egalitarian interpersonal relationships (which are non-existent, in any case) could not fully compensate for the hardships caused by not making enough money to provide adequately for oneself and one's family. I heard a Newton employer speak warmly about Mary Dixon, her domestic of fifteen years, who was "one of the family now," who worries about the employer's husband dressing warmly enough, and whom "we love and trust." I later visited Ms. Dixon's clean but rundown apartment near Franklin Park in Roxbury and heard her talk about her minister's unsuccessful efforts to get her Medicaid coverage (she was fifty-two at the time), about having to make partial payments on her bills again in order to make a vacation trip home to South Carolina, about not declaring two of her six employers in order to be eligible for food stamps, which never seem to get her through to the end of the month. And I realized what this "caring" employer's wages of $3.50 an hour meant to the quality of the domestic's life. Ms. Dixon knew, of course, far better than I:

> Ya, they're all right [her six employers]. As long as I do what I'm supposed to, they're fine. And even then, they don't always do right. Like they go on vacation for two weeks without telling me ahead of time. Or they go for two months in the summer and not even try to help me find some other work. They're not people I consider friends. They're takers. Take as much as you let them. And then grab a little more.

I visited a sixty-four-year-old domestic's apartment heated only by a kitchen stove, and a sick domestic's efficiency heated by only a small space heater. I saw thirty-seven-year-old Edith Lincoln's face when she told me how she'd like to put her daughter in pre-school but because of her financial situation had to leave her with relatives. And I heard domestics' dreams, like Nell Kane's . . .

> I would have liked to get training for better jobs than just domestic work, maybe secretarial work or bookkeeper or something that would be upgrading.

. . . Dorothy Aron's . . .

> If I'd been able to get the education, I would have preferred to teach. I always thought I would be good at that. And I love children. But I just didn't have that opportunity.

. . . and Elizabeth Roy's:

> I always wanted a brick home. I always wanted my family together. But didn't any of that materialize.

In addition to having to cope with low pay, most domestics have experienced or heard about outright cheating by employers. Mary Dixon was one of the domestics who told me about a new practice in the Boston area:

> What's happening now, you have to be careful about checks. I won't take a check on the first day any more. This woman in West Newton was very nice but she gave me a check for thirty-five dollars and it bounced. So I called her and she said I should redeposit the check, she just forgot to put money into her account. So I redeposited it and it bounced again. That's what they're doing today. It's happened to a lot of the girls.

Did you go to her house to get your money?

> No, I didn't have the time for that. They know you're not going all the way back out there. That's why they know they can get away with it. They found a new way to get a free day's work for nothing.

Stories of such trickery are part of the ugly folklore of domestic service. The worst and most pervasive of such practices were apparently during the Depression in the notorious "Bronx slave markets," but stories of cheating by employers persist and are passed around in this labor group, feeding the anger shared among workers toward "these white people." Domestics do not forget employers' abuse of their power even when it is, from the employer's point of view, a minor infraction. Sixty-five-year-old Nell Kane vividly remembered an experience she had in the 1940's:

> She was a wealthy lady. They owned a gladiola farm. I had already learned to cook and serve when I went to work for her. My regular people were away so I went to work for her for the holidays.
>
> From my working in different wealthy homes, I used to write up my own recipes. If I got an idea of something nice to serve, I would build a recipe up and try it. And if it was a success, I'd put it in this little book. I had created a lot of little decorations for their teas and dinners that I had written in there too. Whenever the ideas came, I'd write them down. And whenever you do, it's like a precious little thing that you do because you want to show your work.
>
> And I worked for her and she took my book. I remember her asking the evening I was packing to leave if she could

> borrow the book and copy some of the recipes. I said, "Well, these are the recipes I built from the time I began working and it's kind of precious to me," I said, "but you can take a look at it." My brother drove me out there a few days later to pick it up and she says, "Nell, I've looked everywhere for that book and can't find it." So I looked around but I didn't see it. Do you know, they moved away and I never got that book back. That was one of the most upsetting experiences I've had. That book was so valuable to me. I wanted my children to read it.
>
> I think she took it deliberately. It hurt me. I cried. At that age, I didn't think anyone would do that to you. But some of these women! She had so much more than I did and that little book was my joy. It was a history I would like to have kept.

Telling me this story almost forty years after it happened, Nell Kane once again cried. As Nietzsche said, the *ressentiment*-filled person inevitably becomes "expert in silence, in long memory, in waiting."

Employers' exploiting their advantaged position has been both institutionalized (as in the pay system) and underhanded, both material and psychological. But domestics recognize the exploitation for what it is and know their comparative powerlessness to change it. This knowledge of their powerlessness as a group combines with their inability to express their outrage to those who have caused it to form the basis of the deep and pervasive *ressentiment* in the women I interviewed. The presence of such *ressentiment* attests to domestics' lack of belief in their own inferiority, their sense of injustice about their treatment and position, and their rejection of the legitimacy of their subordination.

Domestics' ways of coping with employers' degrading treatment have been effective, then, in protecting them from the psychological damage risked by accepting employers' belief system but have not been effective in changing the behaviors themselves. All of the behaviors that are generated from the mistress—the demands for various forms of deference, treating domestics as nonpersons or children, the encouragement of unattractiveness and of performances of low intelligence and general incompetence (except for physical labor)—all of these conventions of the mistress-servant relationship have in common the quality of affirming the employer's belief in or of her asking for evidence of the domestic's inferiority. The behaviors and feelings that emanate genuinely from domestics (those not demanded by the mistress) indicate their rejection of the ideas of their own inferiority, of the greater worth of the mistresses, and of the legitimacy of the hierarchical social system.

Domestics do not identify with their employers; they evaluate themselves by criteria other than the society's and their employers' views of those who do domestic work; they show no evidence of considering themselves inferior because of the work they do. But domestics do exhibit the extreme consciousness of the Other that is characteristic of those in a subordinate position; and they do express the *ressentiment* of oppressed who do not accept the justness of their oppression. The elements in the relationship generated by domestics, however, form a weak counterpoint to the deference rituals and maternalism that are the essence of the dynamic between employers and domestics. The employer, in her more powerful position, sets the essential tone of the relationship; and that tone, as we have seen in this and the preceding chapter, is one that functions to reinforce the inequality of the relationship, to strengthen the employer's belief in the rightness of her advantaged class and racial position, and to provide her with justification for the inegalitarian social system.

Notes

Chapter 1

1. See, for example, Shulamith Firestone, *The Dialectic of Sex* (New York: Morrow, 1970), and Juliet Mitchell, *Psychoanalysis and Feminism* (New York: Pantheon, 1974), on sexism; Gordon Allport, *The Nature of Prejudice* (Garden City, N.Y.: Doubleday, 1958), and Joel Kovel, *White Racism: A Psychohistory* (New York: Vintage, 1971), on racism; Wilhelm Reich, *The Mass Psychology of Fascism*, trans. Vincent R. Carfagno (New York: Farrar, Straus & Giroux, 1970), on fascism; Frantz Fanon, *Black Skin, White Masks* (New York: Grove, 1967), and Albert Memmi, *The Colonizer and the Colonized* (Boston: Beacon, 1965), on colonialism; and Herbert Marcuse, *Eros and Civilization* (Boston: Beacon, 1955), and Norman O. Brown, *Life Against Death* (Middletown, Conn.: Wesleyan University Press, 1959), on class domination.

2. Historically, efforts to eliminate domination have never been fully successful, whether small in scale (for example, the nineteenth-century Oneida Community in New York State, the Israeli kibbutzim, or Tanzania's Ujaama villages) or much larger (for example, the U.S.S.R., the People's Republic of China, or Castro's Cuba).

3. This "convention of complexion," which reflects the world stratification system, exists in myriad forms: Southeast Asian women are domestic servants in oil-rich Arab countries; Portuguese domestics serve in Northern Europe; Indians and mestizos serve the "blancos" of Latin America; blacks and "coloreds" serve white South African women; lower-caste (and darker) East Indians serve higher-caste East Indians; and blacks, Japanese, Native Americans, and hispanics in the United States, while less than 20 percent of the population, have comprised approximately half of the domestic servant sector during the twentieth century.

4. Zillah Eisenstein, *Capitalist Patriarchy and the Case for Socialist Feminism* (New York: Monthly Review, 1979), pp. 46–47.

5. This approach to the research was strongly influenced by the thinking of one of my professors in graduate school, Dr. Kurt H. Wolff. See Wolff, *Surrender and Catch* (Hingham, Mass.: Kluwer, 1976). See also Barney Glaser and Anselm Strauss, *The Discovery of Grounded Theory* (Chicago: Aldine, 1967).

6. Allyson Sherman Grossman, "Women in Domestic Work: Yesterday and Today," *Monthly Labor Review,* Aug. 1980, pp. 17–21. It is because of the comparative aspects of my research that I have chosen to retain the terms "domestic" and "servant." Some organizations of household workers in the United States prefer other terms (for example, "household technician" or "household engineer") because they feel the historical connotations of "domestic" and "servant" contribute to the present degraded position of the occupation. However, since these are the terms used in all other parts of the world and by most Americans today, I have retained them throughout this study.

7. This participant observation only as a domestic obviously offered a one-sided perspective and cannot be defended as affording an entirely fair look at the relationship and the two positions that are a part of it. While I could not become a white employer, it may be justifiably argued that my assuming the

position of a black employer might have been valuable in sensitizing me to the concerns of any employer of household help. This form of participant observation, however, was precluded by financial limitations and by my ethical decision not to deceive domestics in any way. (For further discussion of that decision, see note 18 below.)

8. See Robert Merton, *The Focused Interview* (Glencoe, Ill.: Free Press, 1956).

9. American Psychological Association, "Ethical Principles of Psychologists," approved by the Council of Representatives, Jan. 1981, in Paul Davidson Reynolds, *Ethics and Social Science Research* (Englewood Cliffs, N.J.: Prentice-Hall, 1982), p. 154.

10. Ibid., p. 162.

11. American Sociological Association, "Code of Ethics," in Reynolds, *Ethics and Social Science Research*, pp. 164–65.

12. Ibid., p. 166.

13. Ibid., p. 167.

14. Ibid., p. 82.

15. Herbert C. Kelman, "Human Use of Human Subjects: The Problem of Deception in Social Psychological Experiments," *Psychological Bulletin* 67, no. 1 (Jan. 1967): 1–11.

16. Ibid.

17. In fact, with those employers who were dehumanizing, unpleasant, and/or exploitive, I felt some pleasure that I—unlike their previously mistreated domestics—was in a position to use *them*.

18. My answering the ethical question on the basis of social concern led to two additional conclusions: first, that the domestics I studied, having been exploited by more powerful people throughout their lives, would not be deceived by me in any way and, second, that I would try to use my findings to improve the conditions of domestic workers by sharing the research with them, by helping employers become more aware of the effects of their behaviors, and by attempting to call attention to this labor group and its problems in any way I could.

19. Kelman, "Human Use," p. 5.

20. Three well-known studies that exemplify such questionable methods are Stanley Milgram, *Obedience to Authority* (New York: Harper & Row, 1974); Philip Zimbardo, "Pathology of

Imprisonment," *Society* 9 (April 1972): 4–8. and Laud Humphries, *Tearoom Trade: Interpersonal Sex in Public Places* (Chicago: Aldine, 1970).

21. And it does so in precisely the same way the exploitation of domestics reflects and reinforces the class/race/gender hierarchies of the society. Thus my position in relation to the employers had elements in common with their position in relation to domestics. It is no wonder that sociologists can usually be found studying people "they can push around" (Erving Goffman, lecture at Brandeis University, Feb. 24, 1967, as quoted by Barrie Thorne, "Resisting the Draft: An Ethnography of the Draft Resistance Movement," Ph.D. diss., Brandeis University, 1971).

22. Kelman, "Human Use," p. 7.

Chapter 2

1. H. J. Neiboer, *Slavery as an Industrial System* (New York: Lenox Hill, 1971), p. 388.

2. *Encyclopaedia of the Social Sciences* (1937), s.v. "Slavery," by Bernard Stern et al., and Aban Mehta, *The Domestic Servant Class* (Bombay: Popular Books Depot, 1960), p. 4.

3. For an excellent, detailed description of the household slave in Rome, see chapter 2, "In the Household," in R. H. Barrow, *Slavery in the Roman Empire* (London: Methuen, 1928); see also *Encyclopaedia of the Social Sciences*, s.v. "Slavery," p. 77.

4. *Encyclopaedia of the Social Sciences*, s.v. "Slavery," p. 78.

5. Ibid., p. 79.

6. Mehta, *Domestic Servant Class*, p. 8.

7. *Encyclopaedia of the Social Sciences*, s.v. "Slavery," p. 79.

8. Mehta, *Domestic Servant Class*, p. 10.

9. Even into the nineteenth century, it was customary for female servants to be sent with a bride as part of her dowry to the groom's house, where they often became the concubines of the bridegroom. And "female domestic slaves were almost universally kept for sensual purposes" (Mehta, *Domestic Servant Class*, pp. 13–14).

10. Mehta, *Domestic Servant Class*, p. 14.

11. Pamela Horn, *The Rise and Fall of the Victorian Servant* (New York: St. Martin's, 1975), pp. 3–4; Leonore Davidoff and Ruth

Hawthorn, *A Day in the Life of a Victorian Domestic Servant* (London: George Allen & Unwin, 1976), p. 76.

12. Horn, *Rise and Fall*, p. 3.

13. J. Jean Hecht, *The Domestic Servant Class in Eighteenth-Century England* (London: Routledge & Kegan Paul, 1956), pp. 35–38.

14. Ibid., pp. 38–55.

15. Ibid., pp. 60–69.

16. Horn, *Rise and Fall*, p. 5. See also Hecht, *Domestic Servant Class*, p. 69, and Cissie Fairchilds, "Masters and Servants in Eighteenth Century Toulouse," *Journal of Social History* 12, no. 3 (1979): 368–93.

17. Hecht, *Domestic Servant Class*, pp. 187–97, and Charles Booth, *Life and Labour of the People in London* (New York: AMS, 1970), 4: 219–20.

18. Fairchilds, "Masters and Servants," p. 371.

19. And the Roman patriarchal family was in the tradition of the ancient Greek and Hebrew, both of which had cultural origins in northeastern Africa (Max Weber, *Economy and Society*, ed. S. G. Roth and C. W. Wittich [New York: Bedminster, 1968], 3: 1044).

20. Horn, *Rise and Fall*, p. 1.

21. For example, see Leonore Davidoff, "Mastered for Life: Servant and Wife in Victorian and Edwardian England," *Journal of Social History* 7, no. 4 (Summer 1974): 406–28.

22. Fairchilds, "Masters and Servants," p. 372. See also Davidoff, *A Day in the Life*, p. 82.

23. Fairchilds, "Masters and Servants," p. 372.

24. Hecht, *Domestic Servant Class*, pp. 72–101; Fairchilds, "Masters and Servants," p. 379; and Horn, *Rise and Fall*, p. 5.

25. Claude Fleury, as quoted in Fairchilds, "Masters and Servants," p. 372.

26. Weber, *Economy and Society*, pp. 1006–8.

27. Hecht, *Domestic Servant Class*, pp. 75–101; Leonore Davidoff, "Above and Below Stairs," *New Society* 24, no. 551 (1973): 181–83; Ronald Dennis Perry, "The History of Domestic Servants in London, 1850–1900," Ph.D. diss., University of Washington, 1975, p. 48; and for descriptions of cases of extreme abuse, see Horn, *Rise and Fall*, pp. 118–21, and Perry, "History of Domestic Servants," p. 48.

28. Theresa McBride, *The Domestic Revolution* (New York: Holmes & Meier, 1976), pp. 11–12 and 35–36.

29. Ibid., p. 36.

30. David Chaplin, "Domestic Service and Industrialization," in *Comparative Studies in Sociology*, ed. Richard Tomasson (Greenwich, Conn.: JAI, 1978), p. 98.

31. Ibid.

32. McBride, *Domestic Revolution*, p. 19.

33. Adeline Daumard, *Les Bourgeois de Paris au XIX[e] siecle* (Paris: n.p., 1970), as quoted in McBride, *Domestic Revolution*, p. 18.

34. Perry, "History of Domestic Servants," p. 13.

35. Horn, *Rise and Fall*, p. 18.

36. Hecht, *Domestic Servant Class*, p. 7.

37. Davidoff, "Mastered for Life," p. 143.

38. Hecht, *Domestic Servant Class*, p. 4.

39. Davidoff states: "By the 1850's middle-class families, often in imitation of the upper-class round of Court, Balls and the London Season, began to expect more complicated meals and household routines. . . . The size of the houses and the quantity of furniture, crockery, cutlery, curtains, carpets and knick-knacks considered appropriate to one's station increased steadily. Thus there was a demand for more servants" (*A Day in the Life*, p. 75). And Perry elaborates: "Members of that class displayed 'all the paraphernalia of gentility—large and expensive houses, numerous domestic servants employed out doors as well as in, carriage and horses, fairly long holidays abroad, public school and university for the sons of the family, frequent and lavish dinner parties, and so on'" ("History of Domestic Servants," p. 18, quoting J. A. Banks and Olive Banks, *Feminism and Family Planning in Victorian England* [Liverpool: Liverpool University Press, 1964], p. 12).

40. Hecht, *Domestic Servant Class*, p. 9.

41. McBride, *Domestic Revolution*, p. 38, and Hecht, *Domestic Servant Class*, pp. 14–16.

42. Perry, "History of Domestic Servants," p. 57.

43. In nineteenth-century England, for example, there were domestic servants from Ireland, Scotland, continental Europe, Africa, America, and Asia (Hecht, *Domestic Servant Class*, pp. 16–19).

44. In the late nineteenth century, as the supply of domestics began to diminish, it became a common practice in London to force orphans, deserted or wayward children, and those under the Poor

Law Unions into domestic work. Thus not all domestics were in their positions voluntarily. See Perry, "History of Domestic Servants," pp. 59–61, and Davidoff, *A Day in the Life,* p. 36.

45. Hecht, *Domestic Servant Class,* p. 11; Perry, "History of Domestic Servants," pp. 59 and 112–17; McBride, *Domestic Revolution,* p. 48.

46. McBride, *Domestic Revolution,* p. 39. See also David Chaplin, "Domestic Service as a Family Activity and as an Occupation During Industrialization," paper presented to the International Sociological Association, Varna, Bulgaria, Sept. 1970. Cissie Fairchilds also notes the important relationship between feminization and monetization of domestic work: "Without the 18th century monetization of servants' work, the feminization of domestic service which took place in the 19th century would have been impossible. Only when servants were actually paid would the salary differentials between male and female servants make maidservants so much more attractive to employers" ("Masters and Servants," p. 387).

47. Chaplin, "Domestic Service and Industrialization," p. 104.

48. Ibid., p. 104.

49. Booth, *Life and Labour,* p. 212.

50. McBride, *Domestic Revolution,* p. 19, and Chaplin, "Domestic Service and Industrialization," p. 105.

51. Davidoff summarizes some of the deference behavior: "The servant would never sit in the presence of a member of the family or guest, never offer an opinion, never instigate a greeting: in other words, he or she never initiated action as a person" ("Above and Below Stairs," p. 16). The use of the livery for female domestics began in the early nineteenth century but did not become commonplace until mid-century. See Horn, *Rise and Fall,* p. 12.

52. McBride, *Domestic Revolution,* p. 29.

53. Davidoff, "Mastered for Life," p. 416.

54. Ibid., and Perry, "History of Domestic Servants," p. 6.

55. Davidoff, "Mastered for Life," p. 417.

56. McBride, *Domestic Revolution,* p. 116.

57. Chaplin, "Domestic Service and Industrialization," p. 100. Chaplin further notes that the Scandinavian countries were particularly slow in supporting the position of domestics as "freely contracted employees."

58. McBride, *Domestic Revolution,* pp. 113–14.

59. Ibid., p. 115.

60. In England, 400,000 workers left domestic service for factory work during World War I (Davidoff, "Mastered for Life," p. 417).

61. A sample of the Latin American countries surveyed by Ester Boserup makes this clear. See Table 1, page 241.

62. Ester Boserup, *Women's Role in Economic Development* (New York: St. Martin's, 1970), p. 187.

63. Elizabeth Jelin, "Migration and Labor Force Participation of Latin American Women: The Domestic Servants in the Cities," *Signs* 3, no. 1 (1977): 129–41.

64. Margo Lane Smith, "Institutionalized Servitude: The Female Domestic Servant in Lima, Peru," Ph.D. diss., Indiana University, 1971, pp. 94–95.

65. Adriana Marshall, as quoted in Jelin, "Migration and Labor Force Participation," p. 139.

66. Emily M. Nett, "The Servant Class in a Developing Country: Ecuador," *Journal of Interamerican Studies* 8 (1966): 437–52.

67. Nett, "Servant Class," pp. 443–44.

68. Ibid.

69. David Chaplin, "Domestic Service and the Rationalization of Household Economy," unpub. paper 1968, p. 8.

70. Smith, "Institutionalized Servitude," pp. 15–17.

71. Boserup, *Women's Role,* p. 103.

72. For a detailed history of domestic servitude in India before the modern period, see Mehta, *Domestic Servant Class,* pp. 8–14.

73. W. H. Moreland, *India at the Death of Akbar* (Delhi: Atma Ram, 1962), p. 87. Note that the "time of Akbar" was the beginning of the seventeenth century. Moreland states explicitly that "in the towns and cities, slaves were employed for . . . domestic purposes" (p. 84).

74. Table 2 illustrates this. See page 241.

75. Boserup, *Women's Role,* pp. 187–92.

76. The figures in Table 3 (page 241) illustrate the increase in domestic servants in the city of Bombay. Also note that although the occupation was still predominately male, women were increasing at a higher rate than are men: in 1931, 15 percent of the

TABLE 1

Country	Women in Private Domestic Service as % of: All Women in Non-Agricultural Occupations	Women in Private Domestic Service as % of: Total Labor Force in Private Domestic Service
El Salvador	26	97
Costa Rica	34	100
Columbia	37	94
Chile	35	92
Venezuela	26	94
Dominican Republic	22	92
Puerto Rico	13	94

Source: Ester Boserup, *Women's Role in Economic Development* (New York: St. Martin's, 1970), pp. 102–4 and 179.

TABLE 2

Country	Women in Private Domestic Service as % of: All Women in Non-Agricultural Occupations	Women in Private Domestic Service as % of: Total Labor Force in Private Domestic Service
India	5	36
Thailand	5	78
Malaya	17	98
Taiwan	6	65
Hong Kong	26	57

Source: Ester Boserup, *Women's Role in Economic Development* (New York: St. Martin's, 1970), p. 102.

TABLE 3

Year	*Total No. of Domestics*	*No. of Male Domestics*	*No. of Female Domestics*	*% of Total Persons in Industry and Service*
1921	42,555	33,695	8,860	5.8
1931	40,297	34,117	6,180	6.9
1941	47,900	39,000	8,900	6.9
1951	86,875	65,784	21,091	7.0

Source: Aban Mehta, *The Domestic Servant Class* (Bombay: Popular Books Depot, 1960), pp. 40–42.

domestics in Bombay were female; by 1941, 19 percent were; and in 1951, 25 percent.

77. Boserup, *Women's Role,* p. 192.

78. Mehta, *Domestic Servant Class,* p. 47. Note that for his study, Mehta interviewed 500 domestic servants (240 men, 260 women) aged fifteen to seventy years working in all parts of Bombay.

79. Mehta, *Domestic Servant Class,* pp. 159–98.

80. Boserup, *Women's Role,* pp. 104 and 186–93.

81. Jacklyn Cock, *Maids and Madams* (Johannesburg: Ravan, 1980), p. 252.

82. Eleanor Preston-Whyte found in her study of a lower-income area of Durban (housing artisans, clerks, old age pensioners, and 10 percent unemployed) that 30 percent hired casual labor once or twice a week ad hoc; 63 percent employed one full-time or part-time servant; and 7 percent had two servants ("Race Attitudes and Behaviour: The Case of Domestic Employment in White South African Homes," *African Studies* 35, no. 2 [1976]: 71–89).

83. The historical discussion is based on Cock, *Maids and Madams,* pp. 173–228.

84. Cock, *Maids and Madams,* p. 174.

85. Ibid., p. 231, and Michael G. Whisson and William Weil, *Domestic Servants: A Microcosm of "The Race Problem"* (Johannesburg: South African Institute of Race Relations, 1971), pp. 45–47.

86. And because the respondents in this study were all involved in social action or research, the author considered her sample "more liberal and understanding than the norm" (F. E. Streek, *Domestic Servants: A Study of Conditions of Domestics Employed by Border Members of the Black Sash* [Beacon Bay: Black Sash, 1974], pp. 2, 30.)

87. Whisson and Weil, *Domestic Servants,* pp. 7 and 12–29.

88. A Rand is approximately U.S. $.95.

89. Cock, *Maids and Madams,* pp. 28–29 and 41–47.

90. See Preston-Whyte, "Race Attitudes and Behaviour," pp. 77 and 84, and Cock, *Maids and Madams,* p. 99.

91. Whisson and Weil, *Domestic Servants,* pp. 35–38.

92. Cock, *Maids and Madams,* pp. 87–103. However, Preston-Whyte found that lower-income and Afrikaaner employers incorporated more intimacy and protection into their relationships

with domestics than did higher-income English and Jewish employers ("Race Attitudes and Behaviour," pp. 75–79).

93. Whisson and Weil, *Domestic Servants,* p. 47.

94. Ibid., p. 40.

95. Lucy Maynard Salmon, whose classic study was done in 1897, identified the first two periods as stated. I have extended her third period and added the "modern," the justification for which follows. See Lucy Maynard Salmon, *Domestic Service* (New York: Arno, 1972), p. 16.

96. Salmon, *Domestic Service,* p. 16.

97. Velasco, minister of Spain to England, as quoted in ibid., p. 17.

98. *Encyclopaedia of the Social Sciences* (1937), s.v. "Domestic Service," by Amey E. Watson.

99. Salmon, *Domestic Service,* p. 51.

100. Ibid., pp. 39–51.

101. *Encyclopaedia of the Social Sciences,* s. v. "Domestic Service, p. 198.

102. For a full discussion of the "help" arrangement, see Blaine Edward McKinley, "The Stranger in the Gates: Employer Reactions Toward Domestic Servants in America, [illegible]–1875," Ph.D. diss., Michigan State University, 1969, pp. 57–58.

103. For a full discussion of the factors contributing to the "temporary disuse" of the term "servant," see Salmon, *Domestic Service,* pp. 67–100.

104. Daniel Sutherland, *Americans and Their Servants: Domestic Service in the United States from 1800 to 1920* (Baton Rouge: Louisiana State University Press, 1981), pp. 4–6.

105. W. E. B. Du Bois, *The Philadelphia Negro* (New York: Schocken, 1967), p. 136.

106. Sutherland, *Americans and Their Servants,* p. 4.

107. McKinley, "Stranger in the Gates," p. 278.

108. For a detailed discussion of what motivated these groups to emigrate and the United States to encourage immigration, see Salmon, *Domestic Service,* pp. 62–65.

109. Sutherland, *Americans and Their Servants,* p. 49.

110. To many Americans of the nineteenth century, only Protestants were real Christians. Because of the predominance of the Irish in domestic service in the Northeast, McKinley devotes

an entire chapter to a discussion of Irish servants. See McKinley, "Stranger in the Gates," ch. 5.

111. McKinley, "Stranger in the Gates," pp. 152, 155, and 160.

112. The proper behavior of servants was based on the European model: the servant was to remain silent unless spoken to, never sit in the presence of her employer, be as invisible as possible, et cetera. See McKinley, "Stranger in the Gates," pp. 213–14.

113. Sutherland, *Americans and Their Servants,* pp. 30–34.

114. During the 1880's males increased by 73,000, mainly in the multi-servant households of the very wealthy (Sutherland, *Americans and Their Servants,* pp. 14–15). It should be kept in mind, however, that throughout the nineteenth and twentieth centuries in the United States, females were consistently over 90 percent of all domestics.

115. Even in the nineteenth century, there were American critics who considered the occupation "undemocratic" and suggested it be eliminated altogether. Notable were William Alcott and Charlotte Perkins Gilman. To my knowledge, there was no comparably radical thought among European reformers. See Sutherland, *Americans and Their Servants,* pp. 158 and 184.

116. In some areas, being Irish, Indian, or Chinese made one ineligible; in almost all areas of the country, being black did so.

117. For a full discussion of the social and technological changes affecting domestic service around the turn of the century, see Sutherland, *Americans and Their Servants,* pp. 182–99.

118. Sutherland, *Americans and Their Servants,* p. 185.

119. David Katzman, *Seven Days a Week: Women and Domestic Service in Industrializing America* (New York: Oxford University Press, 1978), p. 48.

120. George J. Stigler, *Domestic Servants in the United States, 1900–1940* (Occasional Paper no. 24; New York: National Bureau of Economic Research, 1946), pp. 6–9.

121. Historically, Irish, German, and Scandinavian women have been far more likely to go into domestic service than Russian, Polish, Italian, or Jewish. Katzman speculates that this relates to the cultural matrix of their homelands. Irish women had a long tradition of domestic service; it had been the single most prevalent occupation of women in Ireland. On the other hand, Italian,

Polish, Russian, and Jewish women had not worked outside their homes in Europe. As immigrants, Italian women preferred taking in laundry and Jewish women preferred piecework in the needle trades, both of which allowed them to earn money working at home (Katzman, *Seven Days a Week*, pp. 68–69).

122. Katzman, *Seven Days a Week*, pp. 62–63.

123. I am indebted to Evelyn Nakano Glenn and David Chaplin for stimulating my thinking about the two functions of domestic service. See Glenn, "Occupational Ghettoization: Japanese American Women and Domestic Service, 1905–1970," unpub. paper, 1980, and Chaplin, "Domestic Service and the Negro," *Blue Collar World*, ed. Arthur Shostak and William Gomberg (Englewood Cliffs, N.J.: Prentice-Hall, 1964).

124. This pattern applies to other Third World groups as well as blacks. Latinas, Asians, and Native American women are all disproportionately represented in the domestic servant sector. For example, writing of the work experience of Japanese-American women, Glenn states: "For almost 70 years, from 1905 to 1970, domestic service was the most common form of paid employment for Japanese immigrant women and their daughters" ("Occupational Ghettoization," p. 1). See also Glenn, "The Dialectics of Wage Work: Japanese American Women and Domestic Service, 1905–1940," *Feminist Studies* 6, no. 3 (1980): 432–71.

125. Stigler, *Domestic Servants in the United States*, p. 3, and Allyson Sherman Grossman, "Women in Domestic Work: Yesterday and Today," *Monthly Labor Review*, Aug. 1980, pp. 17–21.

126. Donald J. Treiman and Kermit Terrell, "Women, Work, and Wages: Trends in the Female Occupation Structure," in *Social Indicator Models*, ed. Kenneth Land and Seymour Spilerman (New York: Russell Sage Foundation, 1975), p. 160.

127. Grossman, "Women in Domestic Work," p. 19.

128. For a discussion of the NCHE's activities, see David Katzman, "Domestic Service: Women's Work," in *Women Working*, ed. Ann Stromberg and Shirley Harkess (Palo Alto, Calif.: Mayfield, 1978), pp. 387–89. The NCHE can be contacted at 500 East 62nd Street, New York, N.Y. 10021.

Chapter 3

1. As previously stated, "private household work," as the occupation is termed by the U.S. Census Bureau, includes a number of categories of workers: launderers and ironers, cooks, housekeepers, child care workers, and cleaners and servants. However, because the last category ("cleaners and servants") contains the largest proportion of all female domestics and because all of my domestic interviewees had spent most of their professional housework careers as cleaners, this is the type of work on which this chapter focuses (U.S. Department of Commerce, Bureau of the Census, *Detailed Occupation and Years of School Completed by Age, for the Civilian Labor Force by Sex, Race, and Spanish Origin: 1980 Census of the Population,* Supplementary Report [Washington, D.C.: U.S. Government Printing Office, March 1983], p. 22; and Allyson Sherman Grossman, "Women in Domestic Work: Yesterday and Today," *Monthly Labor Review,* Aug. 1980, p. 20).

2. One domestic, May Lund, received eight dollars an hour from one of her five employers. Her other employers paid her six dollars an hour—the highest pay any of the other interviewees received.

3. Since 1951, private household workers who earn a minimum of fifty dollars from an employer in a quarter are eligible for coverage under the Social Security Act (U.S. Department of Labor, *Women Private Household Workers: A Statistical and Legislative Profile,* [Washington, D.C.: U.S. Government Printing Office, 1958], p. 5).

4. One employer, Marna Houston, had given her housecleaner old clothes on a few occasions, "but I always had the feeling she resented it. So I didn't do it too much. For example, if I gave her a coat, I never saw it on her." And Karen Edwards received a similar impression: "I used to offer the cleaning people kids' clothes but I learned early on at a certain point it came to be viewed as demeaning. So I stopped."

Chapter 4

1. Specifically, they lived in Newton, Wellesley, Belmont, Weston, Wayland, Brookline, Needham, Watertown, Winchester, Arlington, and Boston.

2. I worked in Needham, Wellesley, Belmont, Weston, Cambridge, Wayland, and Dedham.

3. I was also interviewed by Italian and Irish women but did not take those positions because the women worked every day.

4. See particularly Albert Bandura, *Social Learning Theory* (Englewood Cliffs, N.J.: Prentice-Hall, 1973), and Walter Mischel, *Introduction to Personality* (New York: Holt, Rinehart & Winston, 1971), and "Toward a Cognitive Social Learning Reconceptualization of Personality," *Psychological Review* 80 (1973): 252–83.

5. Albert Bandura, "Influence of Models' Reinforcement Contingencies on the Acquisition of Imitative Responses," *Journal of Personality and Social Psychology 1* (1965): 589–95.

6. Daniel Sutherland, *Americans and Their Servants: Domestic Service in the United States from 1800 to 1920* (Baton Rouge: Louisiana State University Press, 1981), p. 10.

7. Elliot Currie, Robert Dunn, and David Fogarty, "The Fading Dream: Economic Crisis and the New Inequality," in *Crisis in American Institutions,* ed. Jerome H. Skolnick and Elliot Currie (5th ed.; Boston: Little, Brown, 1982), p. 92.

8. R. H. Barrow, *Slavery in the Roman Empire* (London: Methuen, 1928), p. 25.

9. Leonore Davidoff, "Mastered for Life: Servant and Wife in Victorian and Edwardian England," *Journal of Social History* 7, no. 4 (Summer 1974): 412.

10. Sutherland, *Americans and Their Servants,* p. 14.

11. Ibid., p. 15.

12. David Katzman, "Domestic Service: Women's Work," in *Women Working,* ed. Ann Stromberg and Shirley Harkness (Palo Alto, Calif.: Mayfield, 1978), pp. 62–63.

13. One domestic's mother had assisted her husband on their farm in South Carolina.

14. For example, the anger expressed by this college-educated professional black woman whose mother had been a life-long domestic (and father, a chauffeur) suggests that the strength of

her reaction to her mother's life might have helped push her away from emulation:

"Her loyalty [to the employing family] bothered me because I didn't think she was treated that well. They gave her the 'you're so wonderful' thing and no money. She would take a lot of crap. Most of the crap she took was long hours. She would leave in the morning before 7:00 and it would be 8:00 or 9:00 at night when she got home. And had nothing [to show for it] but the idea that she worked for [a prominent family]. They had manipulated her into believing that that was an honor.

I thought the hours were unreasonable. I thought going in the back door was unreasonable. There was no lighted path to the back door. And they didn't even clean it when they cleaned the snow away.

My mother didn't retire until she was seventy-two. She loved working for them. She enjoyed their home! I couldn't see that. They were all old together and she felt she'd become part of the family. I said, 'Mother, that is *not* your family. It's never going to *be* your family!' She could not see that. I had to stop talking about it; she thought I was ashamed of her being a domestic."

15. The one domestic not of rural or small town background was born in Boston.

16. This "cushioning" should not be overemphasized, however. Such migrations always entail a kind of cultural shock; for live-in domestics, the problems of adjustment at a new locale may be exacerbated by their feeling alien even where they live. The narratives compiled by Robert Hamburger in *A Stranger in the House* (New York: Macmillan, 1978) illustrate these difficulties movingly.

17. Theresa McBride, *The Domestic Revolution* (New York: Holmes & Meier, 1976), p. 48.

18. I use this word with reservations ever since I asked eighty-two-year-old Anne Ryder at what age she had retired from domestic work and she patiently explained to me: "On that kind of job, you don't 'retire'; you *stop*. 'Retirement' means you get some kind of pay!"

19. This is consistent with the findings from much larger samples. The director of the largest homemaking agency in the Boston area—which employs over four hundred people at any given time—said his average employee had an eighth-grade

education (interview). And according to the 1970 census, private household workers nationally had a median educational level of 8.6 years (U.S. Department of Commerce, Bureau of the Census, *Occupation by Industry* [Washington, D.C.: U.S. Government Printing Office, 1972]).

20. This is not to suggest that race is insignificant. These women found themselves on the lowest economic rung in the South because they were black and, even within domestic service, there exists a hierarchy based on race.

21. Allyson Sherman Grossman, "Women in Domestic Work: Yesterday and Today," *Monthly Labor Review*, Aug. 1980, p. 20.

22. Ms. Owens' observations about Roxbury stores have applicability to stores in low-income areas throughout the country. See David Caplowitz, *The Poor Pay More* (New York: Free Press, 1967).

Chapter 5

1. Albert Memmi, *Dominated Man* (New York: Orion Press, 1968), p. 169.

2. David Katzman, "Domestic Service: Woman's Work," in *Women Working*, ed. Ann Stromberg and Shirley Harkness (Palo Alto, Calif.: Mayfield, 1978), p. 382.

3. Erving Goffman, "The Nature of Deference and Demeanor," *American Anthropologist* 58 (1956): 473–502.

4. Ibid., p. 479.

5. Ibid., p. 475.

6. Some of the younger domestics were clearly struggling with this aspect of their work. May Lund, for example, has recently begun to introduce herself to prospective employers as "Mrs. Lund" and has deliberately stopped using "Ma'am."

7. Goffman, "Nature of Deference and Demeanor," pp. 477 and 481.

8. This is part of the tradition, of course, of servitude in Western Europe and the United States. But whereas the tradition has some flexibility in the North, it was and is quite rigid in the South, and this appears to be related to the close caste-occupation association in the South. A black domestic wrote in 1912: "No

white person, not even the little children just learning to talk, no white person in the South ever thinks of addressing any negro man or woman as Mr., or Mrs., or Miss. In many cases our white employers refer to us, and in our presence, too, as their 'niggers'. No matter what they teach their children to call us—we must tamely submit and answer when we are called" ("More Slavery at the South: By a Negro Nurse," *Independent* 72 [Jan. 25, 1912]: 196–200).

9. Michael G. Whisson and William Weil, *Domestic Servants: A Microcosm of "The Race Problem"* (Johannesburg: South African Institute of Race Relations, 1971), p. 39.

10. The narratives in John L. Gwaltney's *Drylongso* (New York: Vintage, 1981) illustrate aspects of the alternative value system of some Afro-Americans.

11. Goffman, "Nature of Deference and Demeanor," p. 481.

12. Georg Simmel, *The Sociology of Georg Simmel*, ed., trans., and intro. Kurt H. Wolff (New York: Free Press, 1950), p. 321.

13. Goffman, "Nature of Deference and Demeanor," p. 481.

14. David Chaplin, "Domestic Service and the Negro," *Blue Collar World*, ed. Arthur Shostak and William Gomberg (Englewood Cliffs, N.J.: Prentice-Hall, 1964), p. 540.

15. Ibid.

16. See Joel Kovel, *White Racism: A Psychohistory* (New York: Vintage, 1971), ch. 6.

17. Goffman, "Nature of Deference and Demeanor," p. 489.

18. Jacklyn Cock, *Maids and Madams* (Johannesburg: Ravan, 1980), p. 103.

19. David Lockwood, "Sources of Variation in Working Class Images of Society," *Sociological Review* 14, no. 3 (1966): 249–67.

20. In addition to Lockwood, see Cock, *Maids and Madams*, and Howard Newby, *The Deferential Worker* (Madison: University of Wisconsin Press, 1979).

21. Hortense Powdermaker, "The Channeling of Negro Aggression by the Cultural Process," *American Journal of Sociology* 48, no. 6 (May, 1943): 750–58. This discussion of the psychological rewards to the "Uncle Tom" for her performance should not lead the reader to the conclusion that these rewards lessen the performer's sense of exploitation, that they indicate a total victory, or that there are no costs. Religion may placate the victim

of oppression but it does not erase her awareness of the oppression or lessen the anger caused by it. The "Uncle Tom" performance is a performance of the powerless that pleases those who keep them without power. The costs to the giver of this involuntary gift, the capitulation to the desires of one's oppressor, are at least as great as the rewards; any victory for the "Tom" is indeed pyrrhic.

22. Powdermaker, "Channeling of Negro Aggression," p. 754.

23. James Baldwin, *The Fire Next Time* (New York: Dial, 1963), p. 114.

24. Trudier Harris, *From Mammies to Militants* (Philadelphia: Temple University Press, 1982), pp. 15–16.

25. Max Weber, *Economy and Society*, ed. S. G. Roth and C. W. Wittich (New York: Bedminster, 1968), p. 1008.

26. David Katzman and Bonnie Thornton Dill are the only writers I encountered who described the relationship as maternalistic. Katzman states: "In nearly all cases in domestic service both employer and employee were women . . . between the Civil War and World War I. The benevolent role which some employers assumed toward their servants during this period could rightfully be termed 'maternalism'" (Katzman, *Seven Days a Week: Women and Domestic Service in Industrializing America* [New York: Oxford University Press, 1978], p. 153). The rich narratives included in Dill's dissertation illustrate her contention that, in the white employer–black employee arrangement, "race . . . does appear to have modified the maternalistic aspect of the employer-employee relationship." See Dill, "Across the Boundaries of Race and Class: An Exploration of the Relationship Between Work and Family Among Black Female Domestic Servants," Ph.D. diss., New York University, 1979, p. 14.

27. Eli Zaretsky, *Capitalism, The Family and Personal Life* (New York: Harper Colophon, 1973).

28. Leonore Davidoff, "Mastered for Life: Servant and Wife in Victorian and Edwardian England," *Journal of Social History* 7, no. 4 (Summer 1974): 412.

29. Katzman, "Domestic Service," p. 385.

30. See Ann Oakley, *The Sociology of Housework* (New York: Pantheon, 1974).

31. This psychodynamic is similar to that described by

Winthrop Jordan and Joel Kovel. Both convincingly argue that blacks have been used as "contrast conceptions" to strengthen and unify white America. See Jordan, *White Over Black* (Baltimore: Penguin, 1968), and Kovel, *White Racism.*

32. See especially Nancy Chodorow, *The Reproduction of Mothering* (Berkeley: University of California Press, 1978), and Carol Gilligan, *In A Different Voice* (Cambridge: Harvard University Press, 1982).

33. Nancy Chodorow, "Family Structure and Feminine Personality," *Women, Culture and Society,* ed. Michelle Rosaldo and Louise Lamphere (Stanford, Calif.: Stanford University Press, 1974), p. 44.

34. David Chaplin, "Domestic Service and Industrialization," in *Comparative Studies in Sociology,* ed. Richard Tomasson (Greenwich, Conn.: JAI, 1978), p. 100.

35. See the discussions of Latin America, India, and South Africa in Chapter 2.

36. Emily M. Nett, "The Servant Class in a Developing Country: Ecuador," *Journal of Interamerican Studies* 8 (1966): 444.

37. For a full description of the "Bronx Slave Markets," see Ella Baker and Marvel Cooke, "The Bronx Slave Market," *The Crisis* 42, no. 11 (Nov. 1935): 330–31 and 340.

38. Simmel wrote: "It is necessary (above all) to realize that personal action among men by means of things—as, for instance, in robbery and gift, the primitive forms of property exchange—becomes objectified in exchange. Exchange is the objectification of human interaction." (*Sociology,* pp. 387–88).

39. Barry Schwartz, "The Social Psychology of the Gift," *American Journal of Sociology* 73, no. 1 (July 1967): 1–11.

40. Ibid., p. 8.

41. Marcel Mauss, *The Gift* (Glencoe, Ill.: The Free Press, 1954), pp. 72 and 63.

42. Whisson and Weil, *Domestic Servants,* pp. 41 and 43.

43. Ibid., p. 43.

44. Schwartz, "Social Psychology of the Gift," p. 1.

45. Ibid., p. 2.

46. Ibid., p. 3.

47. Pamela Rubovits and Martin L. Maehr, "Pygmalion Black and White," *Journal of Personality and Social Psychology* 25, no. 2 (1973): 210–18.

48. Ibid., p. 217.

49. See, for example, Robert Rosenthal and Lenore Jacobson, *Pygmalion in the Classroom: Teacher Expectation and Pupil's Intellectual Development* (New York: Holt, Rinehart & Winston, 1968); and P. C. Rubovits and M. L. Maehr, "Pygmalion Analyzed: Toward an Explanation of the Rosenthal-Jacobson Findings," *Journal of Personality and Social Psychology* 19 (1971): 197–203.

50. Harris, *Mammies to Militants,* p. 13.

51. It should be remembered, however, that more often than not these transgressions led to dismissal. See the section entitled "Being an Employer" in Chapter 4.

52. Jean-Paul Sartre, *Anti-Semite and Jew,* trans. George J. Becker (New York: Schocken, 1965), p. 69.

53. Frantz Fanon, *Black Skin, White Masks* (New York: Grove, 1967), p. 93.

54. Katzman, "Domestic Service," p. 384.

Chapter 6

1. Ralph Ellison, *Invisible Man* (New York: Vintage, 1972), p. 3.

2. Frantz Fanon, *Black Skin, White Masks* (New York: Grove, 1967), p. 139.

3. Erving Goffman, *The Presentation of Self in Everyday Life* (Garden City, N.Y.: Doubleday Anchor, 1959), p. 151. Although the terms "invisible," "non-person," or "object" to describe servants are not synonymous, I will discuss them without distinguishing between the subtle differences in their meaning. This is because writers use the terms differently but are, in my opinion, referring to closely related mental and social processes (for example, Goffman's use of "non-person" is quite similar to Ellison's use of "invisible person").

4. Theresa McBride, *The Domestic Revolution* (New York: Holmes & Meier, 1976), p. 29.

5. David Katzman, *Seven Days a Week: Women and Domestic Service in Industrializing America* (New York: Oxford University Press, 1978), p. 188.

6. Ellison, *Invisible Man,* p. 3; James, Baldwin, *The Fire Next Time* (New York: Dial, 1963), p. 114; Tom Englehardt, "Ambush at Kamikazee Pass," in *Majority and Minority* ed. Norman R. Yetman

and C. Hoy Steele (2nd ed.; Boston: Allyn & Bacon, 1975), pp. 522–31.

7. Albert Memmi, *The Colonizer and the Colonized* (Boston: Beacon, 1965), p. 86.

8. Frantz Fanon, *Wretched of the Earth* (New York: Grove, 1963), pp. 43 and 37.

9. Elsewhere, I have discussed in greater detail the ideas of these three writers on the consciousness of the Other and *ressentiment* of those in a subordinate position. See Judith Rollins, "And the Last Shall Be First: The Master-Slave Dialectic in Hegel, Nietzsche and Fanon," in "The Legacy of Frantz Fanon," ed. Hussein A. Bulhan, unpub. manuscript.

10. Friedrich Nietzsche, *The Birth of Tragedy and the Genealogy of Morals,* trans. Francis Golffing (New York: Doubleday Anchor, 1956), p. 171.

11. Fanon, *Black Skin, White Masks,* pp. 212–13.

12. G. W. F. Hegel, *The Phenomenology of Mind,* trans. J. B. Baillie (New York: Harper Colophon, 1967), p. 234.

13. Albert Memmi, *Dominated Man* (New York: Orion Press, 1968), pp. 178–79.

14. Hegel, *Phenomenology of Mind,* pp. 238–39.

15. Ibid., p. 237. I did not, however, detect dependence in most of the employers I interviewed. This may have been because most had held jobs outside their homes and none currently had full-time domestic help. The few whose personalities suggested dependence were older women of less than good health (including the two widows). Their dependency seemed to stem from these factors rather than overreliance on their domestics.

16. Fanon, *Wretched of the Earth,* p. 45.

17. For a full discussion of aversive and dominant racism, see Joel Kovel, *White Racism: A Psychohistory* (New York: Vintage, 1971), especially ch. 2.

18. Eleanor Preston-Whyte, "Race Attitudes and Behaviour: The Case of Domestic Employment in White South African Homes," *African Studies* 35, no. 2 (1976): 71–89.

19. Ibid., p. 82.

20. Ibid., pp. 86–87.

21. Katzman, *Seven Days a Week,* p. 200.

22. Ibid.

23. Alfred Lindesmith, Anselm Strauss, and Norman Denzin, *Social Psychology* (5th ed.; New York: Holt, Rinehart & Winston, 1977), p. 420.

24. Bruno Bettelheim, *Surviving and Other Essays* (New York: Alfred A. Knopf, 1979), pp. 77–79.

25. Ibid., p. 82.

26. Fanon, *Black Skin, White Masks,* pp. 146–47.

27. Eugene Genovese, *Roll, Jordan, Roll: The World the Slaves Made* (New York: Vintage, 1976), p. 337.

28. The area of employers' lives most frequently criticized by domestics was their childrearing practices. Domestics described seeing children grow up who no longer speak to their parents; a number said their female employers had expressed envy of the respect and caring the domestic's children demonstrated. For a fuller discussion on comparative childrearing practices and the women's views on it, see Bonnie Thornton Dill, "Across the Boundaries of Race and Class: An Exploration of the Relationship Between Work and Family Among Black Female Domestic Servants," Ph.D. diss., New York University, 1979.

29. Lewis Coser, "Introduction," in Max Scheler, *Ressentiment,* trans. William Holdheim (Glencoe, Ill.: Free Press, 1961), pp. 23–24.

30. Scheler, *Ressentiment,* p. 48.

31. Ibid., p. 50.

32. See Lewis Coser, "Servants: The Obsolescence of an Occupational Role," *Social Forces* 52, no. 1 (Sept. 1973): 31–40, and Jean Genet, *The Maids,* trans. Bernard Frechtman (New York: Grove, 1954).

33. John L. Gwaltney, *Drylongso* (New York: Vintage, 1981), p. 6.

INDEX

Africa: domestic service in, 44. *See also* South Africa; Arab countries
American Psychological Association Ethical Principles of Psychologists, 11–12
American Sociological Association Code of Ethics, 11–12
Ancient world: domestic service in, 21–22
Arab countries: domestic service in, 23, 44
Aristocracy, domestic service in: in pre-industrial England and France, 24–29; in industrializing England and France, 31–32
Asian-American domestic servants, 184
Autonomy of domestic work, 79–80

Baldwin, James: on deference behavior, 170; on invisibility of blacks, 211
Bettelheim, Bruno: on identification, 222–23, 224
Black employers, 148–49
Booth, Charles: on servants in nineteenth century London, 35
Boserup, Ester: on servants in Latin America, 39
Bronx slave markets, 191, 230

Cape Verdeans: as homemaker/health aides, 57
Caribbean servants. *See* West Indians
Children: domestics as, 41, 187–89; employers as, 40–41, 215; people of color as, 161
Cleaning services, commercial, 58
Cock, Jacklyn: on deference, 168; on servitude in South Africa, 46
Concubinage. *See* Sexual exploitation of female servants
Confidantes: domestics as, 166–67
Consciousness of the Other, 212–19
Coping mechanisms of domestics, 212–19
Coser, Lewis: and hostility of domestics, 227

Davidoff, Lenore: on deference, 180
Deference: gestural and task-embedded, 167–70; linguistic, 158–63, 249–50n. 8; in nineteenth century, 35, 239n. 51; spatial, 171–73; in the structure of communication, 163–67; use of, 180
Domestic servants: definition of, 8
Du Bois, W. E. B.: on race and servitude, 51
Duties of servants: in middle-class homes of industrializing England and France, 34; in preindustrial England and France, 25–26; in the United States, 63–152 passim

Eisenstein, Zillah: on patriarchal oppression, 7
Ellison, Ralph: on invisibility, 209, 211
Engelhardt, Tom: on dehumanization of Third World people, 211
England, domestic service in, 24–38 passim
Equipment, 69–70
Ethics of deception in research, 11–16, 234–35n. 7, 235n. 18

Fanon, Frantz: on the colonized mind, 160; on consciousness of the Other in colonized people, 216–18; on the dehumanization of the colonized, 211; on identification, 223; on invisibility, 209–10, 212; on the judgments of one's inferior, 167
Feminization: of domestic servants in England and France, 33–34; of domestic servants throughout the world, 59; of employers, 33; and monetization, 239n. 46
France, domestic service in, 24–38 passim

Genet, Jean: and hostility of domestics, 227
Genovese, Eugene: on identification, 223–24
Gift-giving, 78–79, 157, 189–94
Goffman, Erving: on contact taboos, 164; on deference, 157–58; on non-persons, 210

Harris, Trudier: on appearance of domestics, 200–201; on spatial deference, 171–72
Hegel, G. W. F.: on the consciousness of bondsmen, 216, 217, 218
Hierarchy within domestic service: in contemporary Boston, 75–76; in households of the western

European aristocracy, 24–26; in India, 43
Homemaker/health aides, 54
Hours of work: in India, 43; in South Africa, 46; in the United States, 70–72

Identification, 222–25
Immediate gratification in domestic work, 86–87
India: domestic service in, 23, 42–44; slavery in, 23–24; domestics viewed as children in, 188
Indian (Native American) servants. *See* Native American servants
Industrialization: effects on domestic service, 29–38, 238n. 39
Inferiority of domestics, demands of evidence of, 194–203
Interviewees, domestic: attitudes toward housework, 133, 141; description of, 107; how obtained, 10; preferences in work situations, 147–51; reasons for entering domestic work, 108–14
Interviewees, employers: attitudes toward domestic service, 115–17; description of, 93, 117–18; how obtained, 10; preferences in domestic help, 118–22, 127–31; problems with domestic help, 122–26; reasons for employing domestics, 94–107
Invisibility, 157, 207–12
Irish servants in the United States, 51–52

Japanese-American domestic servants, 108

Katzman, David: on employers' attraction to "inferior" domestics, 202–3; on invisibility of servants, 210; on role of employers' husbands, 182–83; on Southern and Northern employers, 220–21
Kelman, Herbert: on the ethics of deception in research, 13–14, 16; on the objectifying of humans, 16

Latin America: domestic service in, 39–42, 44; domestics viewed as children in, 188; migrants from, 57. *See also* Mexican-American domestic servants
Livery: in nineteenth-century England and France, 31, 35; in pre-industrial aristocratic households of England and France, 25; in the United States, 50, 52
Loneliness, 79–83

Maternalism, 157, 173–203, 251n. 26
Mauss, Marcel: on gifts, 192
McBride, Theresa: on feminization of servitude, 33–34
Mehta, Aban: on servitude in India, 23, 43–44
Memmi, Albert: on the dehumanization of the colonized, 211; on the dependency of servants, 216–17
Men as domestic servants: in Africa and the Arab countries, 44; in the ancient world, 21, 22; in India, 42; in industrializing England and France, 32, 33; in the pre-industrial aristocracy of England and France, 24, 25
Mexican-American domestic servants, 108, 184

Migrancy and servitude: from the Caribbean and Latin America to the United States, 57; in India, 42, 43; of interviewees, 107, 111; in Latin America, 39; in western Europe, 32–33; in the United States during the nineteenth-century, 50; vulnerability of migrants, 151, 165
Minimum wage, 56
Modelling: of mothers of domestics, 112–13, 247–48n. 14; of mothers of employers, 98–102
Monotony of domestic work, 83–85
Moslem world, domestic service in, 23, 44

National Committee on Household Employment (NCHE), 10, 58, 144
Native American servants, 49, 50, 108, 184
Nett, Emily M.: on employer-servant relationships in Latin America, 40–41
Nietzsche, Friedrich: on *ressentiment*, 225, 231; on slave ethics and consciousness, 216
Non-humanness: of servants in nineteenth-century western Europe, 36; of Third World people in films, 211. *See also* Invisibility

Occupational ghettoization, 55
Origins of domestic service, 21–24

Parkhurst, Jessie: on identification, 223
Paternalism: as compared to maternalism, 178–79; in the traditional master-servant relationship, 27–29
Patriarchal domination, 28–29
Physical labor in domestic service, 63–70
Physical punishment of servants: in American colonies, 49; in western Europe, 29, 36
Powdermaker, Hortense: on the Uncle Tom performance, 169–70
Preston-Whyte, Eleanor: on South African servitude, 219–20

Relationship, employer-servant: in contemporary Boston, Chapters 5 and 6; in industrializing England and France, 33–38; in pre-industrial Europe, 26–29; in the United States during the nineteenth century, 53
Research, ethics of deception in. *See* Ethics
Ressentiment, 225–31
Reynolds, Paul Davidson: on ethics of deception in research, 12–13

Scheler, Max: on *ressentiment*, 225–26
Schwartz, Barry: on gifts, 194
Serfdom, 22–23
Sexual exploitation of female domestics: in the ancient world, 22; in India, 23, 236n. 9; of interviewees, 150–51; in Islamic world, 23; in pre-industrial Europe, 29; in South Africa, 46
Simmel, Georg: on the discretionary use of language, 163–64; on the social meaning of object exchange, 252n. 38
Slavery: in the ancient world, 21–22; in Christianity, 23; in India,

23; in the Middle Ages, 22; in the Moslem world, 23; as the origin of domestic service, 21–24; in the United States, 24
Social Security, 56, 76–78, 181
South Africa: domestic service in, 44–48; domestics viewed as children in, 188
Southern employers: as compared to Northern employers, 219–22
Status symbols, domestic servants as: in India, 23; in Rome, 22; in the United States, 102, 104–6, 107

Third World, domestic service in, 38–48

"Uncle Tom" performance: of domestics, 167–70; of employers, 182
United Domestic Workers Organization of San Diego, 58
United States, domestic service in: during the colonial period, 48–50; from Independence to mid-nineteenth century, 50–51; from mid-nineteenth century to World War I, 51–54; from World War I to the present, 54–58

Value system of women, 186

Wages: in Boston during the 1960's, 68; in contemporary Boston, 72–76; in pre-industrial England and France, 26
Weber, Max: on patriarchal domination, 28–29
West Indians: as homemaker/health aides, 57; as migrants, 57; problems of, 66, 72, 81
Whisson, Michael G., and William Weil: on gift-giving, 192–93; on servants as "girls," 159–60; on servitude in South Africa, 46–47
Wolff, Kurt H., 15
Women's work, domestic service as, 21–22, 183–84
Work demands of employers, 63–70